TRIED & TRUE RECIPES

For Sportsmen Like You

TRIED & TRUE RECIPES

For Sportsmen Like You

BY HENRY & MARY SINKUS

WILLOW CREEK PRESS®

Published by Willow Creek Press
P.O. Box 147, Minocqua, Wisconsin 54548

For information on other Willow Creek Press titles, call 1-800-850-9453

Printed in The United States of America

TABLE OF CONTENTS

ENTRÉES 79

INTRODUCTION

"My Mother taught me to cook and instilled in me a passion for excellence. My work for major corporations over thirty years exposed me to cultures throughout the world, allowing me to study various cuisines and culinary techniques. I continue my studies every day, experimenting in my own kitchen... I encourage you to be creative in your culinary endeavors and to add a large amount of love to each of your creations. Cooking is an art form. The plate is your canvas; your paint, the products of the earth."

—Henry Sinkus, *The Northwoods Table*

Henry was my husband, my advocate and my life coach. He was a Chef who loved nothing more than walking into his kitchen at home or in his beloved restaurant, Pine Baron's, and creating dishes with flavors from the exotic to the familiar. He liked to say that he learned to cook by watching his Mother and some of the great chefs of the world (Julia Child and Pierre Franey hosted his favorite TV cooking shows).

He felt strongly that cooking was an art form—he never cooked simply for sustenance. Any meal was a production in our home, as in our restaurant. The food had to look as good as it tasted.

Henry was writing his 6th book in 2019. He wasn't able to complete that book before his death. You will find the recipes that he did complete in this book as well as selections from his previous books and those I feel might have been some of his favorites.

Henry left his friends with a basket full of good memories and his readers with an abundance of tantalizing recipes.

I dedicate this book to our Pine Baron's family, our staff—always professional, fiercely loyal, often amusing. You helped make our dream come true.

HENRY'S FAVORITES

CREAM OF WILD MUSHROOM SOUP

SERVES 6-8

INGREDIENTS

- **½ lb. sweet butter**
- **1 small onion, diced**
- **2 cups domestic mushrooms, thickly sliced (about ⅛")**
- **2 cups wild mushrooms (shiitaki, portobello, ceps, etc. Domestic mushrooms may be substituted), thickly sliced (about ⅛")**
- **3 tbsp. sweet butter**
- **¼ cup flour**
- **6 cups chicken stock**
- **2 cups heavy cream**
- **2 tbsp. sherry**
- **¼ tsp. nutmeg**

DIRECTIONS

In a 4 quart stockpot, melt the butter and sauté the onion until translucent. Add the mushrooms and sauté for 10 to 15 minutes, stirring occasionally.

In a 1 quart saucepan, melt 3 tablespoons sweet butter. Add ¼ cup flour and whisk constantly to achieve a light brown roux. Slowly add 2 cups chicken stock. Stir constantly until thickened.

Add remaining 4 cups chicken stock to the sautéed mushrooms and onions. Add the roux mixture and cream and simmer until heated through. Add sherry and nutmeg. Adjust seasoning to taste with salt and freshly ground pepper.

IMAGINE THE FLAVOR AND EARTHY AROMA OF MUSHROOMS FRESH FROM THE FOREST FLOOR AND THE SWEETNESS OF ONION BLENDED WITH SHERRY, CREAM AND A HINT OF NUTMEG–A SOUP FOR THE SOUL.

HENRY CALLED THIS "A SOUP FOR THE SOUL." AS WITH MOST OF HIS CREAM SOUPS, IT WAS LOVINGLY PREPARED WITH AN ABUNDANCE OF BUTTER AND HEAVY CREAM. A COUPLE WHO FREQUENTED OUR RESTAURANT REGULARLY, ALWAYS LOOKED FORWARD TO HAVING ONE OF THESE SOUPS. ONE EVENING, TONY SAID TO HIS WIFE, MARION, "COULDN'T YOU MAKE THIS AT HOME WITH SKIM MILK AND MARGARINE SO IT WOULDN'T HAVE SO MANY CALORIES AND SO MUCH CHOLESTEROL?" MARION REPLIED, "SURE, BUT IT WOULDN'T TASTE ANYTHING LIKE HENRY'S VERSION."

SPICY ROAST DUCKLING WITH RASPBERRY SAUCE

SERVES 2

INGREDIENTS

- 1 duck, split and trimmed of all fat and excess skin
- 2 pieces carrot (5” long)
- 2 pieces celery (5” long)
- 1 cup thinly sliced onion

DRY RUB SEASONING

In a food processor, blend together the following:

- 2 tbsp. salt
- ¼ cup dried onion
- 1 tbsp. cayenne pepper
- 1 tsp. white pepper
- 2 tbsp. paprika
- 2 tbsp. dried basil
- 1 tbsp. dry mustard
- 1 tsp. ground cumin
- 1 tbsp. granulated garlic

RASPBERRY SAUCE

- 8 oz. jar raspberry jam
- 1 cup sugar
- 1 cup water
- 1 oz. Triple Sec
- 1 oz. raspberry brandy
- ½ cup teriyaki sauce
- 2 tbsp. cornstarch

DIRECTIONS

In a 3" deep roasting pan, build a nest of carrot and celery topped with sliced onion. Moisten the duck halves with a commercially-prepped, mild Louisiana-style hot sauce and place the halves atop the vegetables, skin side up. Dust the duck with 1 tablespoon dry rub seasoning, Cover the pan with heavy-duty aluminum foil and bake in a preheated 400 degree oven for 2 hours, 15 minutes.

Remove the duck from the oven and carefully remove foil, avoiding steam. Cool slightly and remove duck to platter. (Note: the fat in the pan can be saved and used for frying potatoes.) Discard the vegetables and any liquid remaining in pan. Cool the duck until it can be comfortably handled. Remove all bones from the body cavity. Wrap each half in plastic wrap and refrigerate overnight.

Prepare sauce by mixing the raspberry jam, sugar, water, Triple Sec and brandy in a 2-quart saucepan. Stirring constantly, bring the mixture to a boil. Reduce heat and simmer for 10 to 15 minutes, stirring occasionally. Strain the mixture into a clean 2-quart saucepan and return to low heat. Mix together cornstarch and teriyaki sauce. Add raspberry jam mixture and heat until slightly thickened.

To serve, remove plastic wrap from duck. Place halves, skin side up, in a baking dish and heat in a 400 degree oven for 15 minutes. Baste with raspberry sauce and return to oven for 5 minutes.

THE SAUCE FOR THE DUCK WAS BORN OF A "CONTEST" BETWEEN HENRY AND WALTER MAZUR, A DEAR FRIEND AND OWNER OF BLUE BAYOU INN IN MANITOWISH WATERS. YES, A CAJUN RESTAURANT IN THE MIDDLE OF THE NORTHWOODS OF WISCONSIN. HENRY AND WALT, BOTH STRONG-WILLED AND DETERMINED, EACH PREPARED THEIR OWN VERSION OF THE SAUCE AND, WHEN TASTING BEGAN, THE ARGUING ENSUED, EACH CHEF EXTOLLING THE CHARACTERISTICS AND ADVANTAGES OF THEIR CREATION. AT THE END OF AT LEAST AN HOUR, I COULD HEAR HENRY SAY "DOESN'T REALLY MATTER WHAT YOU THINK, WALT. IT'S MY RESTAURANT AND IT'S GOING TO BE MY SAUCE!" THE TWO MEN EMERGED FROM THE KITCHEN, OPENED UP A BOTTLE OF WINE AND PROCEEDED TO DISCUSS THE WEATHER.

CRANBERRY CREAM CHEESE

SERVES 6-8

INGREDIENTS

- **1 8-oz. block cream cheese, softened**
- **½ cup cranberry mustard**

DIRECTIONS

Combine the cream cheese with the cranberry mustard, best if done with the aid of an electric mixer.

Place mixture in a serving bowl, refrigerate at least 1 hour before serving. Serve with your favorite crackers or flatbread.

A TRADITION AT PINE BARON'S WAS TO PROVIDE EVERY DINER WITH AN AMUSE-GUEULE THAT CONSISTED OF CRANBERRY CREAM CHEESE, CRUDITE AND FLATBREAD. DEFINITELY THE EASIEST RECIPE HENRY EVER CREATED.

KIMCHEE (SPICY PICKLED CABBAGE)

SERVES 4

INGREDIENTS

- 1 large head cabbage, cored, quartered, and cut into 1" pieces
- 2 large onions, peeled, cut in half and sliced ½" thick
- 2 large carrots, peeled and shredded
- 3 tbsp. minced garlic
- 1 tbsp. fresh grated ginger (optional)
- 2 tbsp. salt
- 2 cups rice wine vinegar
- 1 6-oz. jar kimchee base*
- 1 gallon container with a screw lid

DIRECTIONS

In a large, stainless steel bowl, mix together the vegetables, garlic and salt. Cover the bowl and refrigerate for 12 to 24 hours. Drain the vegetables, return to the bowl, and stir in the kim chee base. With a slotted spoon transfer the vegetable mixture to the gallon container and add the vinegar.

Screw the lid onto the container and shake it to the mix. Store the kim chee in the refrigerator. The kim chee will be ready in 3 to 4 days and will only get better with age.

*If kimchee mix is not available, mix together 2 tbsp. garlic, 2 tsp. salt, 1½ tbsp. red chili flakes, 1 tbsp. sugar, 1 tbsp. grated fresh ginger, and 2 tbsp. red wine vinegar.

Let stand for 1 hour, and then process in a blender or food processor until a smooth paste forms. If too thick add a bit more vinegar.

AN ACQUIRED TASTE, BUT IF YOU LIKE HOT AND SPICY, THIS IS JUST THE TICKET.

HENRY WAS ALWAYS INTRIGUED BY LAKE SUPERIOR WHITEFISH—A COMMODITY EASILY PROCURED FRESH FROM LAKE FISHERMEN TO OUR NORTH ALONG THE SOUTHERN SHORE OF LAKE SUPERIOR.

SMOKED WHITEFISH AND CREAM CHEESE SPREAD

SERVES 4-6

INGREDIENTS

- ½ lb. boneless, skinless smoked whitefish, cut into chunks
- 3 tbsp. onion, chopped
- 1 tbsp. capers
- 8 oz. cream cheese, softened
- few drops hot sauce, to taste

DIRECTIONS

In a food processor fitted with a stainless blade, pulse chop the whitefish, onion and capers until finely minced. Add the cream cheese and process until smooth. Adjust flavor with the hot sauce. Transfer to a serving bowl, cover with plastic wrap and refrigerate at least one hour before serving. Makes about 2 cups.

FOR A SMOOTHER, LESS GRAINY TEXTURE, ADD 2 TABLESPOONS HEAVY CREAM DURING PROCESSING.

SAUERBRATEN

SERVES 6–8

INGREDIENTS

- 3–4 lb. venison roast

MARINADE

- 1 cup dry red wine
- 1 cup red wine vinegar
- 2 cups cranberry juice
- 1 spice bag with 1 tbsp. pickling spice, 2 bay leaves, 6 whole cloves and 10 peppercorns
- 1 medium onion, peeled and sliced

BRAISING LIQUID

- ¼ lb. butter
- ¼ lb. chopped bacon
- 1 cup chopped onion
- 1 cup chopped celery
- 1 cup chopped carrot
- 10 peppercorns, crushed
- 1 cup dry red wine
- ½ cup red wine vinegar
- 2 cups beef or chicken stock

SAUCE FINISH

- ½ cup Knorr Demi-Glace Sauce Mix
- 1 cup braising liquid
- 1 cup finely chopped ginger snap cookies (10–12 cookies)
- 1 cup cream sherry

THIS RECIPE SHOULD BE STARTED 3–4 DAYS BEFORE YOU PLAN TO SERVE IT. SWEET/SOUR CABBAGE AND MASHED POTATOES ARE THE IDEAL ACCOMPANIMENT.

DIRECTIONS

To make the marinade, bring cranberry juice to a boil in a 1-quart saucepan. Add spice bag, remove from the heat and allow to cool. Place venison roast in a 2½ gallon Ziploc bag. Add onions, cooled cranberry juice with the spice bag, red wine and red wine vinegar. Place bag in large bowl or deep pan and refrigerate for at least 2 to 3 days. Rotate and flip the bag 3 times each day.

Preheat oven to 325 degrees.

Remove the roast from the marinade. Wipe off excess moisture and place on a holding tray. Strain marinade, discarding the vegetables and spice bag, reserving the liquid. In a large, deep Dutch oven, melt the butter and brown the roast on all sides. Remove the venison to a holding tray. Add the bacon to the Dutch oven, stir and cook 3 to 4 minutes. Remove and reserve the bacon for the sauce. Add the celery, carrot and onion to the Dutch oven, stirring and cooking for 5 minutes. Return the venison to the Dutch oven. Add the peppercorns, wine, red wine vinegar and stock. Bring to a boil, cover and place in the oven for 2 to 3 hours or until venison is fork tender. Remove from the oven, uncover and cool to room temperature. Strain and discard the vegetables. Reserve the strained braising liquid. Refrigerate the venison and liquid overnight.

Remove excess fat from the surface of the braising liquid. Remove venison and slice ¼" thick and arrange in a decorative baking/serving dish. Heat 1 cup of the braising liquid over medium heat. Whisk in the sauce mix, gingersnaps, and sherry, whisking until the sauce thickens. Spoon sauce over the venison and warm in a 150 degree oven for 15 to 20 minutes.

KÖNIGSBERGER KLOPSE (GERMAN MEATBALLS)

SERVES 4

INGREDIENTS

- 2 slices bread soaked in ½ cup milk
- 1 lb. ground venison
- ½ lb. ground pork
- 2 eggs
- 1 tbsp. butter
- ⅓ cup minced onion
- 3 tbsp. chopped parsley
- ½ tsp. salt
- ¼ tsp. paprika
- ⅓ tsp. fresh lemon zest, chopped
- 1 tbsp. lemon juice
- 1 tbsp. Worcestershire sauce
- 4 anchovy filets, finely chopped (optional)
- Sprinkling of nutmeg
- 6 cups chicken or vegetable stock

THESE MEATBALLS ARE ALSO GREAT AS AN APPETIZER—REDUCE THE SIZE TO 1" (ABOUT 1 OUNCE).

DIRECTIONS

Squeeze the milk from the bread. In a food processor, combine the pork, venison and bread. Pulse chop 3–5 times to combine. Transfer to a large bowl.

In a large skillet, melt the butter and sauté the onion until golden brown. Add to the meat mixture with the remaining ingredients except for the chicken or vegetable stock. Combine well using your impeccably clean hands. Shape into 2" balls. Drop into the boiling stock and simmer, covered, for 15 minutes.

Transfer the meatballs to a baking dish.

The Gravy: For every cup of stock to be made into gravy, prepare the following: In a large skillet, melt 2 tablespoons butter. Whisk in 2 tablespoons flour, cooking and whisking until smooth and thickened. Stir in the cooking liquid, cooking over low heat until thickened. Add 2 tablespoons finely chopped capers and ½ cup sour cream.

Place meatballs in the gravy and reheat over low heat for 15 minutes. Serve over buttered noodles.

THAI COUNTRY-STYLE CURRY

SERVES 6-8

INGREDIENTS

- **2 lbs. ground venison**
- **2 tbsp. vegetable oil**
- **1 cup chicken stock, mixed with 1 tbsp. panang curry paste**
- **2 tbsp. fish sauce**
- **6 basil leaves, shredded**
- **2 cups shredded cabbage**
- **2 medium carrots, shredded**
- **1–2 Thai chili peppers, minced (optional)**
- **1 15-oz. can unsweetened coconut milk**

THAI CHILI PEPPERS CAN BE CHOPPED AND STORED IN PLASTIC BAGS IN THE FREEZER.

DIRECTIONS

Heat the vegetable oil in a wok and stir-fry the venison for 3 to 4 minutes. Add the shredded cabbage and carrot, continue cooking for 4 to 5 minutes. Add the chili pepper (if desired) and stir in the chicken stock curry paste mixture and bring to a boil. Stir in basil leaves, reduce heat and simmer 3 to 5 minutes. Serve over steamed rice.

HENRY EXPERIMENTED ENDLESSLY WITH THAI AND INDIAN CURRIES. FOR MANY YEARS, WE DID A "THAI NIGHT" IN THE RESTAURANT WITH A FIXED MENU AND SOUP, SALAD AND CURRY THAT COULD BE AS SPICY AS DESIRED.

MARINATED FRESH VEGETABLE SALAD

SERVES 2-4

INGREDIENTS

- ⅓ cup red wine vinegar
- ⅔ cup olive oil
- 1 tbsp. lemon juice
- ¼ tsp. basil
- ¼ salt
- ⅛ tsp. white pepper
- 2 cups asparagus tips
- 2 cups domestic mushrooms, thickly sliced
- 1½ cups zucchini squash, ¼" diced
- 2 cups artichoke hearts
- 2–3 tbsp. capers (optional)
- ½ cup sliced black olives (optional)

DIRECTIONS

In a stainless steel bowl, whisk together vinegar, olive oil and lemon juice. Add basil, salt and pepper. Let stand for 20 minutes. Arrange vegetables in a stainless steel or glass bowl. Add marinade and cover with plastic wrap. Refrigerate for 24 hours. Serve on a bed of fresh salad greens.

PLUCK THE FRESHEST VEGETABLES FROM A LAKESIDE FARMER'S MARKET TO MAKE THE CRISP, REFRESHING SALAD. DEFINITELY A DEPARTURE FROM THE ORDINARY.

BREAKFAST SKILLET

SERVES 4-6

INGREDIENTS

- **1 lb. ground venison**
- **8 strips bacon, chopped**
- **½ tsp. smoked paprika**
- **⅛ tsp. white pepper**
- **2 cups hash brown potatoes, raw**
- **6 oz. small curd cottage cheese**
- **6 oz. mixed shredded cheeses (cheddar, mozzarella, Monterey jack)**
- **7 eggs, beaten**

A GREAT DISH FOR A BRUNCH. IF YOU'D LIKE, SPICE IT UP A BIT BY SERVING ANY KIND OF SALSA ON THE SIDE.

DIRECTIONS

In a large skillet or sauté pan, brown the bacon over medium heat. Stir in the venison, paprika and pepper. Cook and stir until the venison is no longer pink. Drain the mixture in a sieve.

In a large bowl, combine all ingredients. Transfer to a buttered baking dish. Bake in a 325 degree oven 40 to 60 minutes until set and browned.

POT-AU-FEU FOR TWO

SERVES 2

INGREDIENTS

- 8–10 oz. venison tenderloin, trimmed of all fat, gristle and silver skin
- 2 boneless chicken thighs
- 6 strips bacon, chopped
- ¼ cup minced onion
- 1 clove garlic, crushed and minced
- 2 cups chicken stock
- 1 cup white wine
- ¼ cup teriyaki sauce
- 6 baby carrots, scraped and trimmed
- 1 turnip, peeled and cut in 1" dice
- 1 leek, white part only, cut in half in 2" sections and washed
- 20 tiny French green beans (haricot vert)
- 6 fresh shitake mushrooms, stems removed
- 10 peppercorns
- 1 bay leaf
- 6 coriander leaves

THE NATURAL PARTNER TO THIS DISH IS THIS TOMATO SAUCE.

TOMATO SAUCE

- 1 tbsp. each of butter and olive oil
- ½ cup chopped onion
- 1 15-oz. can sliced stewed tomatoes, chopped
- Salt and pepper to taste
- 2 tbsp. freshly grated or prepared horseradish (excess moisture removed)
- ½ cup heavy cream

DIRECTIONS

In a 1-quart saucepan, heat the butter and olive oil. Add the onion and garlic and cook until opaque. Add the tomatoes, salt and pepper and bring to a boil. Reduce heat and simmer 5 minutes. Stir in the horseradish and cream. Now all you need is a crisp green salad and a loaf of garlic bread to finish this dish off.

Using a 4-quart Dutch oven, cook the bacon until rendered of all fat. Remove and reserve the bacon. Add the chicken thighs, skin side down, season with salt and pepper and cook 2 to 3 minutes. Add the reserved bacon, onion and garlic and cook for 2 to 3 minutes longer.

Stir in the chicken stock, wine, teriyaki sauce, peppercorns and bay leaf. Bring to almost a boil and add the leeks, carrots and turnips. Cover and simmer 15 to 20 minutes, or until the chicken is cooked and the vegetables are tender crisp. Add the venison, mushrooms and green beans. Cover and continue cooking until the venison is set (springs back from the touch).

Remove the venison and slice into 2 portions. In 2 heated soup plates or pasta dishes, divide the chicken and vegetables and arrange artistically. Top with venison slices and hot broth. Garnish with coriander leaves and tomato sauce on the side.

CATFISH KABOBS

AN INTERESTING TAKE ON KABOBS COOKED ON THE GRILL. HENRY DEVELOPED THIS RECIPE BECAUSE CATFISH HAS ALWAYS BEEN MY FAVORITE FISH.

CATFISH KABOBS

SERVES 4

INGREDIENTS

- 1½ lbs. boneless, skinless catfish fillets,
- cut into 1" cubes
- 12 strips bacon
- 2 small zucchini squash, cut into ½" slices
- 1 sweet red pepper, seeded and cut into 1" squares
- 10" bamboo skewers

BEFORE STARTING YOUR GRILL, REMOVE THE COOKING GRATE AND TREAT WITH A NON-STICK COOKING SPRAY. REPLACE THE GRATE JUST BEFORE YOU START TO GRILL THE KABOBS—THEY'LL HAVE LESS TENDENCY TO STICK TO THE GRILL.

MARINADE

- ⅓ cup olive oil
- zest of ½ lemon
- 3 tbsp. lemon juice
- 3 tbsp. white wine
- ¼ cup fresh dill, chopped
- 1 tablespoon honey
- salt and pepper

DIRECTIONS

Combine the marinade ingredients in a stainless steel bowl. Cover and set aside.

Cut bacon strips in half. Wrap each catfish cube with bacon. Thread a wrapped cube on a skewer followed by a pepper square and a squash slice. Build each skewer to 3 pieces of catfish, pepper and squash.

Place kabobs in a single layer in a shallow pan or dish. Add the marinade. Cover and refrigerate for at least 1 hour.

Grill the kabobs over medium heat for 3 to 4 minutes on each side, basting occasionally with the marinade. Serve with steamed rice.

WILD RICE CAKE

SERVES 6-8

INGREDIENTS

- 2 cups sifted flour
- ¼ tsp. salt
- ½ tsp. baking powder
- 2 cups cooked wild rice (cooked until bloomed)—½ cup uncooked*
- 1 cup walnut pieces
- ½ cup sweet butter
- 1 cup dark brown sugar
- 4 eggs
- ¾ cup buttermilk
- 1 tsp. maple flavoring
- ½ tsp. nutmeg

BOURBON CUSTARD SAUCE

- 2 egg yolks
- 1 cup confectioners' sugar
- 8 tbsp. bourbon
- 1 cup whipping cream
- 1 tsp. vanilla

WILD RICE HAS BEEN A STAPLE IN NORTHERN WISCONSIN FOR AS LONG AS CAN BE REMEMBERED. THIS CAKE COMBINES SOFT AND CRUNCHY TEXTURES WITH SWEET AND NUTTY FLAVORS. AND THE BOURBON CUSTARD SAUCE IS THE PERFECT FINISH.

DIRECTIONS

Combine flour with salt and baking powder.

Combine cooked wild rice with walnut pieces (for a smoother textured cake, process rice and walnuts one or two pulse cycles in food processor with steel blade).

Cream butter until softened. Add brown sugar. Beat in eggs, one at a time. Add buttermilk, maple flavoring and nutmeg. Beat until light and fluffy. Stir in flour mixture until thoroughly mixed. Fold in rice and walnut mixture. Pour batter into an 8" tube or bundt pan. Bake in a 350 degree oven for about 1 hour. Yields one 8" tube cake. Works well topped with bourbon custard sauce.

Bourbon Custard Sauce:
Beat 2 egg yolks and the sugar with a wire whisk until the mixture is a pale yellow. Slowly add the bourbon and mix well. Whip the cream until stiff. Fold in vanilla and then egg mixture into the whipped cream. Makes about 2 cups. Keep refrigerated.

*How to cook wild rice
One cup uncooked wild rice yields four cups cooked.

In a fine strainer, rinse rice under cold water. Place the rice in a heavy saucepan and add 4 cups of water for each cup of rice. Heat to boiling, cover and simmer over low heat for 40 to 50 minutes, until grains begin to split or rice is tender.

MOTHER MARY'S VENISON STEW

SERVES 8

INGREDIENTS

- **3 lbs. venison roast cut into 1" cubes**
- **2 large onions sliced 1" thick and quartered**
- **3 stalks celery, finely chopped**
- **4 carrots, peeled and cut into bite-size pieces**
- **2 large potatoes, peeled and cut into ¾" dice**
- **1 package frozen baby peas**
- **1 15-oz. can tomato sauce**
- **1 tbsp. brown sugar**
- **½ tsp. white pepper**
- **1 tsp. chopped garlic**
- **1 tsp. thyme**
- **1 or 2 bay leaves**
- **2 cups chicken stock**

DIRECTIONS

In a heavy skillet or sauté pan, brown the venison in a small amount of olive oil over medium-high heat in several batches. As the venison browns, transfer it to a 4-quart ovenproof covered casserole.

In the heavy skillet or sauté pan, cook the onions, celery and carrots over medium-low heat for 5 to 6 minutes. Add the cooked vegetables peas and potatoes to the venison in the casserole.

In a large bowl, mix together the remaining ingredients. Add to venison mixture in the casserole and stir well. Cover and bake in a preheated 325 degree oven for 2 to 3 hours or until the venison is fork-tender and the potatoes are cooked. Serve over buttered baked potatoes or pasta.

Pearl onions will formalize this dish. If you like, thicken the stew with 2 tablespoons cornstarch mixed in 1 cup water. On the stovetop, heat the cooked stew to almost boiling. Stir in the cornstarch mixture and continue stirring until the stew has thickened, approximately 3 to 5 minutes.

STEW HAS NEVER BEEN ONE OF MY FAVORITE DISHES. HENRY FELT IF HE NAMED THIS ONE AFTER ME, MY TASTES MIGHT CHANGE. IT WORKED.

APPETIZERS, SIDES & SALADS

WILD MUSHROOM CRISPS

SERVES 2 AS AN APPETIZER

INGREDIENTS

- **1½ cups fresh shredded potato (1 large potato)**
- **2 oz. butter**
- **1 oz. cream cheese, softened**
- **6–8 dried wild mushrooms (domestic mushrooms may be substituted)**
- **Fresh tomato slice**
- **Shredded asiago or mozzarella cheese**
- **Minced fresh herbs—basil, dill, cilantro**

DIRECTIONS

Reconstitute mushrooms in sherry wine. Drain well.

Season potatoes with salt and pepper. Melt 2 ounces sweet butter in a 7" skillet over medium-high heat. Add potatoes, forming a level round disc. Fry 3 to 4 minutes per side or until crispy and brown. Remove from pan and drain on paper towel. To assemble, spread cream cheese on potato crisp. Arrange mushrooms, and top with fresh tomato. Sprinkle minced herbs and cheese on top.

Place the crisp on a baking sheet and cook in a 350 degree oven for 3 to 5 minutes until cheese melts.

THESE HORS D'OEUVRES ARE LITHUANIAN-INSPIRED POTATO PANCAKES TAKEN TO A NEW DIMENSION. THE CRISPS EAT LIKE PIECES OF PIZZA TOPPED WITH FLAVORFUL WILD MUSHROOMS, ONE OF THE EARTHIEST INGREDIENTS FOUND "UP NORTH."

STEWED PUMPKIN AND APPLES

SERVES 4-6

INGREDIENTS

- 4 cups fresh pumpkin or squash, peeled and cut into 1" cubes
- 1 qt. Water
- 4 cups Granny Smith apples, cored and cut into 1" cubes
- 2 tbsp. Craisins (dried cranberries) or raisins
- ⅓ cup sweet butter
- 2 oz. Cointreau
- ½ cup dark brown sugar
- Salt and pepper to taste
- Pinch of ground or fresh ginger

DIRECTIONS

Bring water to boil in a 2-quart saucepan. Add pumpkin and cook until fork or skewer can be inserted without resistance. Drain pumpkin, toss together with apples and Craisins and transfer to an ovenproof casserole.

In a 1-quart saucepan, melt the butter. Add ginger, brown sugar and Cointreau and heat until the sugar is dissolved. Season with salt and pepper and pour over pumpkin apple mixture. Bake, uncovered, in a preheated 300 degree oven for 30 to 40 minutes or until apples are semi-soft. Dot each serving with a pat of butter.

**To create Pumpkin Apple Bisque, process the mixture with 1 quart of heavy cream and 2 cups chicken or vegetable stock in a food processor or blender. Salt and pepper to taste.*

A DELICIOUS ACCOMPANIMENT TO FALL AND WINTER MENUS, THIS SIDE DISH IS A CORNUCOPIA OF REDS AND ORANGES OF AUTUMN LEAVES IN FALL BURST. THE CRAISINS—DRIED CRANBERRIES WHICH ARE INTENSELY SWEET AND CHEWY ENOUGH TO EAT AS A SNACK—PROVIDE THE ZIP OF THE DISH.

VENISON COCKTAIL MEATBALLS

MAKES APPROXIMATELY 48 MEATBALLS

INGREDIENTS

- **2 lbs. ground venison**
- **1 lb. Italian sweet sausage**
- **1 cup grated Parmesan cheese**
- **2 beaten eggs**

SAUCE

- **1 jar currant jelly**
- **1 cup barbecue sauce (use your favorite)**

DIRECTIONS

In a large bowl, combine all meatball ingredients. Mix well and form into teaspoon-size balls. Place the meatballs on a non-stick baking pan. Bake in a preheated 350 degree oven for 20 to 30 minutes or until cooked through.

Combine the sauce ingredients in a medium saucepan and heat through. Pour over the meatballs in a serving dish or transfer the meatballs and sauce to a slow cooker set at low for service.

VENISON SALAMI

MAKES 3 ROLLS

INGREDIENTS

- 5 lbs. course ground venison
- 2 lbs. course ground pork shoulder
- 1½ tbsp. course ground pepper
- 2½ tsp. garlic powder or granulated garlic
- 1½ tsp. barbecue seasoning
- 5 tsp. Morton's Tender Quick Salt
- 1½ tsp. hickory smoked salt
- 1½ tsp. onion flakes

DIRECTIONS

In a large, stainless steel bowl, mix all ingredients well, cover and refrigerate for 24 hours. Repeat the mixing and refrigeration process each day for 3 days.

Shape the venison mixture into 3 rolls. Place on an oiled rack in a shallow pan, and bake at 150 degrees for 6 to 7 hours. Remove excess cooking juices as necessary, Cool the salami, wrap in plastic, and store under refrigeration.

This salami can be frozen, and is best if vacuum packaged.

A GREAT ITEM FOR A CHRISTMAS OR HOUSE GIFT. YOU CAN ADD ADDITIONAL FLAVOR BY SMOKING THE SALAMI FOR ABOUT 1 HOUR.

WALLEYE MOUSSE

SERVES 6-8

A QUICK AND EASY APPETIZER. TO COOK THE WALLEYE, USE YOUR MICROWAVE.

INGREDIENTS

- **½ pound cooked walleye**
- **¼ cup heavy cream**
- **2 tbsp. chives**
- **2 tbsp. red onion, minced**
- **2 tbsp. fresh lemon juice**
- **salt and pepper**

DIRECTIONS

In a food processor fitted with a stainless blade, pulse chop the fish, chives, onion and lemon juice. With the processor running, slowly pour in the cream, and process until the mixture thickens, 1 to 2 minutes. Season with salt and pepper to taste.

Place the mousse in a serving dish. Cover and refrigerate at least 2 hours. Serve with whole wheat crackers or toast rounds.

WHITEFISH LOUIS

SERVES 4-6

QUICK, HEALTHY AND DELICIOUS. THE PERFECT MEAL FOR WARM SUMMER NIGHTS.

INGREDIENTS

- **3 cups cooked whitefish, flaked**
- **2 cups sliced iceberg lettuce**
- **2 cups sliced romaine lettuce**
- **2 Roma tomatoes, cut into wedges**
- **2 hard boiled eggs, sliced**
- **¼ cup sliced black olives**

DRESSING

- **¾ cup mayonnaise**
- **4 tbsp. ketchup**
- **⅓ cup sour cream**
- **2 tbsp. heavy cream**
- **2 tbsp. green onion, sliced**
- **1 tbsp. sweet pickle relish**
- **1 tsp. lemon juice**
- **1 tsp. Worcestershire sauce**

DIRECTIONS

In a medium bowl, combine all dressing ingredients and mix well. Cover and refrigerate for at least 1 hour.

Mix lettuce and arrange on a service plate. Mound fish in the center. Arrange tomato wedges, egg slices and olives around the fish. Ladle half the dressing over the fish. Serve remaining dressing on the side.

LITHUANIAN-STYLE MASHED POTATOES

SERVES 4

INGREDIENTS

- **4 cups diced red potatoes, cooked and bashed**
- **1 large white onion, peeled, chopped and sautéed in ¼ lb. butter until brown**
- **8 strips of bacon, cooked and chopped fine**
- **½ cup shredded white cheddar cheese**
- **⅓ cup heavy cream**
- **¼ tsp. white pepper**
- **2 tsp. salt**

DIRECTIONS

In a large bowl, combine all the ingredients and mix thoroughly.

Place the potato mixture in a buttered ovenproof dish, cover with foil, and bake in a preheated 300 degree oven for 1 hour or until hot.

A LIGHTER VERSION OF A POTATO CASSEROLE CALLED KUGULA.

TANGY VENISON MEATBALLS IN CREAMY HORSERADISH SAUCE

SERVES 4-6

INGREDIENTS

- 1 cup rye breadcrumbs
- ¼ cup milk
- 1 egg, beaten
- 1 tsp. salt
- ¼ tsp. pepper
- ¼ lb. bacon, finely chopped
- 2 tbsp. prepared white horseradish
- 1 ½ lbs. ground venison
- 2 tbsp. vegetable oil
- 2 tbsp. flour
- 13 oz. beef broth
- 1 cup sour cream

DIRECTIONS

Preheat oven to 350 degrees. In a large bowl, combine the breadcrumbs, milk, egg, salt, pepper, venison, bacon and 1 tbsp. horseradish. Mix thoroughly.

Using a tablespoon, form meatballs and transfer to a 9"x13" non-stick baking pan. Bake for 20 minutes. Dust the meatballs with flour and transfer to a large skillet or sauté pan to which you have added the vegetable oil.

Set the burner to medium heat. Add the beef broth, and gently stir until sauce is thickened. Mix in the sour cream and 1 tbsp. horseradish and stir until thoroughly combined. Do not boil.

When the sauce has thickened, remove from heat and serve with egg noodles.

FRESH BERRY NAPOLEONS

SERVES 6

INGREDIENTS

- 1 pint blueberries
- 1 pint strawberries, sliced
- 1 pint blackberries
- 1 pint raspberries
- 2 tbsp. Triple Sec
- 11"x15" commercially prepared puff pastry sheets cut into 3" rounds;
- 1 lb. mascarpone cheese, softened (cream cheese may be substituted)
- 2 tbsp. rum
- 1 tbsp. raspberry liqueur
- 1½ cups heavy cream
- ¼ cup granulated sugar

BERRY PICKERS FLOCK TO THE NORTHWOODS EACH SUMMER, SHARING THE TERRITORY WITH FRUIT-LOVING BEARS. LAYER FRESH BERRIES INTO THE RICH INGREDIENTS OF THIS RECIPE FOR A LYRICAL FRUIT SENSATION THAT WILL AMAZE YOUR GUESTS.

DIRECTIONS

Place the puff pastry rounds on a baking sheet. Prick each with a fork. Moisten with a pastry brush dipped in cold water and sprinkle with sugar. Bake in a preheated 400 degree oven for 10 to 15 minutes, or until brown and crispy. Remove to a rack and cool completely.

Toss together blueberries, strawberries and blackberries. Add the Triple Sec. Refrigerate at least one hour.

In a stainless steel bowl, using an electric mixer, blend together the cheese, sugar, rum, and raspberry liqueur. Slowly add the cream until you achieve the consistency of butter cream frosting. Transfer the mixture to a pastry bag fitted with a #22 open star tip.

To assemble, pipe a dot of cheese mixture in the center of each dessert plate. Gently press a puff pastry round on the cheese to secure the base. Pipe a band of cheese mixture on the edge of the puff pastry round. Fill the center with fruit mixture. Repeat this process with two more layers. Garnish the plate with fresh raspberries.

ITALIAN-STYLE BLUEGILL APPETIZERS

MAKES 30 APPETIZERS

USE COMMERCIALLY PREPARED PESTO AND STORE ANY UNUSED PORTION AS SEASONING IN YOUR NEXT ITALIAN DISH.

INGREDIENTS

- ½ pound boneless, skinless bluegill fillets, cooked and flaked
- 1 loaf french bread (baguette), sliced diagonally into 30 pieces
- 4 tbsp. butter, softened
- 1 roasted red pepper, cut in fine strips
- 1 roasted yellow pepper, cut in fine strips
- 1 tbsp. olive oil
- 2 garlic cloves, crushed and minced
- ½ small onion, minced
- 2 tbsp. capers
- ⅓ cup sliced black olives
- 2 tbsp. pesto sauce
- 2 tbsp. lemon juice
- salt and freshly ground black pepper to taste
- chopped fresh parsley

DIRECTIONS

Lightly butter the baguette slices. Place them, butter side up, on a baking sheet and bake in the center of a 325 degree oven for 10 to 12 minutes, or until lightly browned.

In a heavy skillet, heat the oil and sauté the onion and garlic until soft. Remove from heat and add the peppers, capers, olives, pesto and lemon juice. Mix in the fish and season to taste with salt and pepper.

Spread about 2 teaspoons of the fish mixture on each baguette slice. Garnish with chopped fresh parsley.

MOLDED LAKE TROUT SALAD

SERVES 6

INGREDIENTS

- **1½ cups lake trout, cooked and flaked**
- **1 15-oz. can pineapple chunks, drained, saving ¼ cup of the liquid**
- **½ cup celery, diced**
- **1 red apple, unpeeled, cored and diced**
- **¼ cup black olives, chopped**
- **1 envelope unflavored gelatin**
- **1 tbsp. cold water**
- **¾ cup boiling water**
- **1 tbsp. lemon juice**
- **1 cup mayonnaise**
- **salt to taste**
- **chopped lettuce**

DIRECTIONS

Combine fish, pineapple, celery, apple and olives in a mixing bowl. In a separate bowl, mix the gelatin with 1 tablespoon cold water. Add the boiling water and stir until gelatin is dissolved. Add the liquid from the pineapple and the lemon juice.

Combine the gelatin mixture with the mayonnaise and stir into the fish mixture. Add salt to taste. Pour into a lightly-oiled mold and refrigerate for at least 6 hours. Unmold on a bed of chopped lettuce.

FOR A MORE ROBUST FLAVOR, SUBSTITUTE WHITE WINE FOR THE WATER IN THE GELATIN. THE WINE CAN BE EASILY HEATED IN THE MICROWAVE.

VENISON SALAD

SERVES 10

INGREDIENTS

- **½ lb. venison, roasted to medium rare, sliced into thin strips 3" long and 1" wide**
- **10 bib lettuce leaves, shredded into ½" strips**
- **1 cup Italian salad dressing**
- **10 coriander leaves, shredded**
- **6 mint leaves, shredded**
- **1 stalk lemongrass (use only the bottom 2") minced**
- **1 red onion, sliced into thin rings**

DIRECTIONS

Place venison in a glass pie plate. Cover the venison with 1 cup dressing. Cover the pie plate with plastic wrap and refrigerate at least 2 hours.

To assemble the salad, divide the lettuce among 10 plates. Drain the dressing from the venison and arrange the strips in the center of each plate. Garnish with coriander, mint, lemongrass and red onion.

SALMON MACARONI SALAD

SERVES 6

FOR A TROPICAL FLAVOR, SERVE ON PINEAPPLE SLICES. THIS SALAD IS HEARTY ENOUGH TO BE SERVED AS A COLD ENTRÉE ON A WARM SUMMER DAY.

INGREDIENTS

- **3 cups cooked macaroni or other small pasta shape**
- **1 lb. poached salmon fillet**
- **3 boiled eggs, chopped**
- **2 stalks celery, chopped**
- **1 10-oz. package frozen baby peas**
- **1 medium onion, chopped**
- **1 green pepper, seeded and chopped**
- **3 green onions, sliced and chopped**

DRESSING

- **⅓ cup creamy Italian dressing**
- **1 cup mayonnaise**
- **½ cup sour cream**
- **½ tsp. granulated garlic**
- **½ tsp. salt**
- **⅛ tsp. white pepper**

DIRECTIONS

In a small bowl, mix together the dressing ingredients and refrigerate for 1 hour.

In a large bowl, mix together the salad ingredients. Fold in the dressing.

LOMI LOMI SALMON (HAWAIIAN LUAU SALMON)

SERVES 6-8

INGREDIENTS

- 2 cups salt-cured or gravlax salmon, skin removed and cut into ½" dice
- 3 Roma tomatoes, seeded and cut into ½" dice
- 1 medium sweet onion, diced
- 2 green onions, thinly sliced

DIRECTIONS

Mix all ingredients and serve in a bowl placed in a larger bowl of crushed ice.

FOR A MORE FORMAL PRESENTATION, REDUCE THE DICE SIZE TO 1/4-INCH. CUT THE TOPS FROM CHERRY TOMATOES, REMOVE THE PULP AND DRY THE TOMATO SHELLS. FILL THE TOMATOES WITH THE SALMON MIXTURE.

BAKED VENISON SUMMER SAUSAGE

MAKES 4 LBS.

INGREDIENTS

- **3 lbs. ground venison**
- **2 lbs. ground beef**
- **1 tbsp. granulated garlic**
- **1 tbsp. granulated onion**
- **3 tbsp. kosher salt**
- **1½ tsp. black pepper**
- **1½ tsp. white pepper**
- **2 tbsp. smoked paprika**
- **1 tbsp. whole mustard seed**
- **1 cup ice water**
- **1 tbsp. liquid smoke**
- **1 tsp. Morton's Tender Quick**

DIRECTIONS

Mix together the venison and beef. In a medium bowl, combine all dry seasonings. Stir in the water, liquid smoke and Tender Quick. Add to the ground meat and mix thoroughly for 3 to 4 minutes. Cover the bowl and refrigerate 1 to 2 days.

Divide the meat mixture into 4 equal portions. Shape into logs about 2" in diameter and 10" to 12" long. Wrap the logs tightly with plastic wrap, tying the ends. Then wrap with foil. Place on a rack over a drip pan and bake in a 350 degree oven for 1½ hours.

Remove the logs from the oven and cool for 1 hour. Remove the foil and plastic wrap and place the rolls on several layers of paper towel to drain. Rewrap with plastic wrap and foil for storage in the freezer. To serve, remove the plastic wrap and foil. Thaw and thinly slice. Serve with crackers or cocktail rye.

VENISON MAC

SERVES 6

THIS DISH SHOULD APPEAL TO ALL AGES AND CAN BE PREPARED AHEAD (UP TO THE POINT OF BAKING) SO YOU CAN SPEND YOUR TIME ENJOYING YOUR FAMILY AND FRIENDS.

INGREDIENTS

- **3 tbsp. olive oil**
- **1½ lbs. ground venison**
- **½ lb. bulk pork sausage**
- **1 medium onion, chopped**
- **2 stalks celery, thinly sliced**
- **1 green pepper, seeded, sliced and chopped**
- **1 tsp. garlic, chopped**
- **¼ tsp. nutmeg**
- **¼ tsp. salt**
- **¼ tsp. pepper**
- **½ tsp. oregano**
- **1 small can sliced black olives**
- **2 15-oz. cans stewed tomatoes, chopped**
- **1 lb. elbow macaroni, cooked according to package directions**
- **½ lb. grated mozzarella cheese**

DIRECTIONS

Preheat oven to 350 degrees.

In a large Dutch oven, heat the olive oil over medium heat and brown the venison and pork sausage. Stir in the onion, celery, green pepper and garlic. Cook until the onions are translucent.

Mix in the nutmeg, salt, pepper, oregano and black olives. Add the stewed tomatoes and simmer for 30 minutes. Mix in the cooked macaroni and 1 cup of the cheese.

Transfer to a greased baking dish and bake for 25 minutes. Top with the remaining cheese and bake an additional 15 to 20 minutes until cheese is melted and begins to brown.

SOUPS, STEWS & CHOWDERS

BASIC FISH STOCK

YIELDS ABOUT 3 1/2 QUARTS

INGREDIENTS

- 3–4 lbs. fish heads, bone and fins from lean fish (avoid oily fish like salmon and trout)
- 4 tbsp. olive oil
- 1 large onion, thinly sliced
- 3 stalks celery, thinly sliced
- 4 carrots, peeled and thinly sliced
- 1 fennel bulb and fronds, thinly sliced
- 1 bunch parsley, chopped
- 2" piece of ginger, peeled and thinly sliced
- 3 whole bay leaves
- 2 garlic cloves, crushed
- 1 tsp. dried thyme
- 1 tsp. dried rosemary
- 2 cups white wine
- cold water
- celery salt

FREEZE SOME OF THE STOCK IN ICE CUBE TRAYS FOR RECIPES CALLING FOR A SMALL AMOUNT OF THE STOCK. 1 CUBE EQUALS ABOUT 1/4 CUP.

DIRECTIONS

Wash the fish heads, bones and fins under cold water. Remove and discard the gills as they will make the stock taste bitter.

In a tall stockpot, heat the olive oil on high. Add the fish heads, bones and fins and reduce the heat to medium. Stir for 5 to 6 minutes or until slightly browned. Add the vegetables and continue to cook until the onions are limp and opaque.

Stir in the wine, herbs and enough cold water to cover everything by 2". Bring the stock to a simmer. Do not boil or the stock will turn cloudy. Simmer for 60 minutes.

Remove from the heat and allow to rest for 20 to 30 minutes. Strain the stock through a mesh strainer lined with cheesecloth or a basket-type coffee filter. If using a coffee filter, gently stir the stock in the strainer to speed the straining process. Discard all the filtered material. Add celery salt to the stock as desired.

After the stock has cooled, pour into 1-quart containers, leaving 1" for expansion. Cover and freeze.

CAMP STEW

SERVES 10-12

INGREDIENTS

- 3 to 4 lbs. venison cut into 1½" cubes
- ¼ lb. butter
- ½ cup olive oil
- 3 tbsp. chopped garlic (12 cloves)
- ½ cup Worcestershire sauce
- 6 serrano peppers or 3 jalapeño peppers, seeded and chopped
- ½ tsp. white pepper

STOCK

- 3 cups beef broth
- 3 cups chicken stock
- 1 bottle red wine
- 4 carrots, peeled and sliced
- 1 16-oz. package frozen peas
- 1 10-oz. package frozen corn
- 2 onions, peeled, sliced and quartered
- 1 10-oz. package frozen green beans
- 1 lb. mushrooms, quartered
- 2 15-oz. cans sliced stewed tomatoes
- 8 medium red potatoes, quartered

ROUX

- 3 tbsp. butter
- 3 tbsp. flour

DIRECTIONS

In a large frypan or sauté pan, melt ⅓ of the butter and oil over medium-high heat. Add the venison in batches, browning on all sides. Add additional butter and oil as needed.

Move the browned meat to a large bowl. Mix together the garlic, Worcestershire sauce, peppers and white pepper. Stir this mixture into the meat.

In a large stockpot, combine the beef broth, chicken stock and red wine. Heat to almost a boil. Add the carrots, peas, corn, onion, green beans, mushrooms, stewed tomatoes and venison. Bring to a slow boil. Reduce heat, cover and simmer for 1½ hours. Add the potatoes and cook for an additional hour.

Prepare the roux by mixing together the melted butter and flour. Place 2 cups of liquid from the stew in a small pot. Slowly add the roux, whisking constantly. Return this mixture to the large pot and cook until the potatoes are tender and the stew has thickened.

FOR A ZESTIER FLAVOR, SUBSTITUTE THREE CANS OF DARK BEER FOR THE RED WINE.

SPANISH RAGOUT OF VENISON

SERVES 6-8

INGREDIENTS

- 3 lbs. venison, cut into 1" cubes
- 1 cup pitted prunes
- 1 cup dried apricots
- 1 cup sherry
- 1 cup pitted Kalamata olives
- 1 jar roasted red peppers, drained and chopped
- ¼ cup red wine vinegar
- ¼ cup olive oil
- 1 small jar capers
- 3 tbsp. minced garlic
- 1 tbsp. dried oregano
- 1 tsp. hot chili powder
- 1 tbsp. smoked paprika
- 2 15-oz. cans stewed tomatoes, chopped
- 1 cup dry white wine
- ⅓ cup brown sugar
- 2 cups chicken stock

THICKENER

- 1 tbsp. red wine vinegar
- 3 tbsp. water
- 2 tbsp. flour

THIS RAGOUT HAS WONDERFUL FLAVORS AND CAN BE FROZEN FOR A SPECIAL MAKE-AHEAD MEAL.

DIRECTIONS

In a large stainless steel bowl, mix together the venison, olives, peppers, vinegar, oil, capers (including liquid), garlic, oregano, chili powder and paprika. Cover and refrigerate overnight.

Place the apricots and prunes in a glass or ceramic bowl with the sherry. Cover and refrigerate overnight.

Preheat oven to 325 degrees. In a 6–8 quart Dutch oven, combine the venison and apricot/prune mixtures. Mix in the tomatoes, white wine, brown sugar and enough chicken stock to just cover the mixture. On the stovetop, bring the mixture to a boil. Cover and place in the oven. Bake for 1 hour. Remove the cover and continue baking for 35 minutes. Cool to room temperature and refrigerate overnight.

Remove any fat on the surface and reheat on the stovetop over medium heat, stirring occasionally, until the mixture comes to a boil. Stir in the thickener, reduce heat and simmer, stirring occasionally, until thickened.

COLD BEET SOUP

SERVES 6-8

INGREDIENTS

- 2 15-oz. cans diced beets, drained, juice reserved
- 8 oz. sour cream
- 1 qt. beef or vegetable stock
- 8 oz. heavy cream
- ⅓ cup white vinegar
- 3 tbsp. minced chives
- 1 medium cucumber, peeled, seeded and julienne sliced
- 2–3 tbsp. minced fresh dill

DIRECTIONS

In a large stainless steel bowl or 4-quart stockpot, blend together the sour cream and beet juice. Slowly incorporate the beef or vegetable stock, then blend in the heavy cream and vinegar. Add beets, cucumber, chives and dill, and mix gently. Refrigerate at least two hours before serving.

This soup should be piquant and slightly sweet in taste. Adjust the seasoning with salt and additional vinegar if required.

IN THIS REFRESHING CHILLED SOUP, THE OFTEN NEGLECTED BEET IS FINALLY GIVEN ITS DUE. INSTEAD OF BEING SLICED AND SERVED AS A LONELY SIDE DISH, THE BEETS IN THIS RECIPE PROVIDE THE ROSY PINK COLOR AND TANGY FLAVOR OF THE PERFECT FIRST COURSE FOR ANY SUMMER MENU.

BLACK BEAN AND VENISON SOUP

SERVES 6-8

INGREDIENTS

- 2 tbsp. butter
- 2 tbsp. olive oil
- 1 large onion, sliced and chopped
- 2 medium carrots, shredded
- 2 stalks celery, sliced
- 2 medium green peppers, chopped
- 1 lb. ground venison
- 4 cups beef broth
- 1 tsp. oregano
- 2 tbsp. tomato paste
- 1 bay leaf
- ½ tsp. red pepper flakes
- 1 tbsp. smoked paprika
- 1 16-oz. can stewed tomatoes
- ½ cup sherry (optional)
- 2 tbsp. lemon juice (optional)
- 3 cans black beans, drained

DIRECTIONS

Heat the butter and olive oil in a large soup pot or Dutch oven. Add the onion, carrot, celery and green pepper. Cover and cook over medium heat until softened. Add the venison and beef broth and stir to break up the meat. Cook until meat is no longer pink.

Stir in the oregano, tomato paste, bay leaf, red pepper flakes, smoked paprika and stewed tomatoes and sherry and lemon juice, if desired. Add the black beans and stir well. Simmer until heated through. Adjust seasoning with salt and red pepper flakes.

TEXICAN VENISON MEATBALL SOUP

SERVES 6-8

INGREDIENTS

- 2 tbsp. olive oil
- 1 large onion, coarsely chopped
- 2 medium carrots, coarsely chopped
- 2 medium zucchini, coarsely chopped
- 2 garlic cloves, chopped
- 2 tbsp. chopped green chilis (may use canned)
- 4 cups beef broth
- 1 14-oz. can Italian stewed tomatoes, coarsely chopped, reserve liquid
- 1 tsp. marjoram
- ½ tsp. ground cumin
- ¼ tsp. white pepper
- 1 cup fresh or frozen corn
- ¼ cup uncooked rice
- 1 egg
- 2 tbsp. cilantro, chopped
- 2½ tsp. chili powder
- 1 tsp. salt
- 1 lb. ground venison
- ½ lb. bulk pork sausage

DIRECTIONS

Heat olive oil in a large non-reactive Dutch oven. Add onion, carrot, zucchini, garlic and green chilis. Cover and cook over medium heat, stirring often, until vegetables are softened, 8 to 10 minutes.

Add beef broth, tomatoes with their juice, marjoram, cumin, white pepper. Bring to a simmer, reduce heat to low and simmer 1 hour. Stir in the corn.

In a medium saucepan with lightly salted boiling water (use rice cooking instructions for amount of water), cook rice 5 minutes. Drain and rinse under cold water. This can be done while the beef broth mixture is simmering.

In a medium bowl, stir together the rice, egg, cilantro, chili powder and salt until well blended. Add the ground venison and bulk pork sausage. Mix well.

Roll mixture into meatballs about the size of a tablespoon. Drop into simmering soup, increase heat to high and return soup to a simmer. Reduce heat to low and simmer, stirring gently, until meatballs are cooked through, 15 to 20 minutes.

Serve with corn chips and sriracha sauce for those who like it hot.

THAI VENISON & RICE SOUP

SERVES 4-6

INGREDIENTS

- **1 lb. coarsely ground venison**
- **5 slices thick-cut bacon, finely chopped**
- **1 egg**
- **4 cups chicken stock**
- **2 cups cooked rice**
- **2 tbsp. fish sauce**
- **4 lettuce leaves, finely shredded**
- **3–4 slices fresh ginger, peeled and minced**
- **3 green onions, finely sliced**
- **¼ tsp. ground white pepper**
- **brown sugar and teriyaki sauce to taste**

DIRECTIONS

Mix together the venison, bacon and egg. Form into ¾" balls. In a large saucepan, bring the chicken stock to a boil and carefully add the meatballs. Cook until firm and cooked through, 6 to 8 minutes. Add the rice and fish sauce. Stir in the lettuce, ginger, green onion and white pepper. Season to taste with brown sugar and teriyaki sauce.

CREAMED CORN AND VENISON SOUP

SERVES 6-8

INGREDIENTS

- **2 tbsp. butter**
- **1 scallion, minced**
- **2 tsp. minced fresh ginger**
- **2 lbs. ground venison**
- **3 17-oz. cans creamed corn**
- **3 cups chicken broth**
- **3 tbsp. teriyaki sauce**
- **1 tbsp. dry sherry**
- **1 tbsp. cornstarch**

DIRECTIONS

Heat butter in a large saucepan or Dutch oven over medium-high heat. Add scallion and ginger. Stir-fry until fragrant, about 30 seconds. Add venison and stir-fry until no longer pink, about 3 minutes.

Stir in creamed corn, chicken broth, teriyaki sauce and sherry. Reduce heat to low and simmer 20 minutes.

Dissolve cornstarch in a small bowl with 2 tablespoons water. Add to the simmering soup and cook until thickened, about 3 minutes.

VENISON CHILI WITH CHORIZO SAUSAGE

SERVES 6-8

INGREDIENTS

- **2 lbs. ground venison**
- **1 medium onion, peeled, sliced and quartered**
- **2 tsp. minced garlic**
- **1 lb. cooked chorizo sausage, cut in half lengthwise and sliced**
- **¼ cup brown sugar**
- **4 tbsp. chili powder**
- **1 tsp. ground cumin**
- **3 15-oz. cans stewed tomatoes**
- **1 jar of your favorite spaghetti sauce**

DIRECTIONS

In a 4-quart Dutch oven, brown the venison in 1 tablespoon of olive oil. Add the garlic and onion. Reduce heat and simmer until the onions are opaque. Add the remaining ingredients. Simmer for 1 to 1½ hours. Adjust seasoning to taste with salt and pepper.

LEFTOVER CHILI CAN BE USED FOR TOPPING ON SAUSAGE SANDWICHES OR HOT DOGS.

HOT AND SOUR FISH SOUP

SERVES 4

THIS MAKES A GREAT DIET MEAL—VERY LOW IN CALORIES. THAI CURRIES AND HOISIN ARE AVAILABLE AT MOST LARGE SUPERMARKETS.

INGREDIENTS

- **1 lb. boneless, skinless catfish fillets, cut into 1" pieces**
- **2 medium zucchini, thinly sliced**
- **1 jalapeño pepper, seeded and finely chopped**
- **1 tbsp. olive oil**
- **1 large onion, peeled, sliced and chopped**
- **1 tsp. red Thai curry paste**
- **1 package frozen baby peas, thawed**
- **2 tsp. lime juice**
- **4 tbsp. hoisin sauce**
- **2 packages chicken-flavored ramen noodles**
- **2 tbsp. Thai fish sauce**

DIRECTIONS

Cook the ramen noodles according to package directions. Keep warm.

Heat the oil in a large sauté pan or wok and stir-fry the onion until opaque. Stir in the curry paste, jalapeño pepper, zucchini and peas. Reduce heat to medium-low and stir-fry for 3 to 5 minutes or until zucchini is just cooked. Stir in the catfish, lime juice, hoisin sauce, fish sauce and 2 cups of the noodle broth. Bring to a boil, reduce the heat to low and simmer until the fish is cooked, about 3 to 5 minutes.

Divide the warm noodles among 4 serving bowls and top with equal portions of the soup.

VENISON, SPLIT PEA AND LENTIL SOUP WITH BACON DUMPLINGS

SERVES 4-6

INGREDIENTS

- ½ lb. dried split peas
- ½ lb. lentils
- 4 tbsp. butter
- 1 medium onion, finely chopped
- 2 medium carrots, finely chopped
- 2 stalks celery, finely chopped
- 8 cups chicken stock
- 2 medium Yukon gold potatoes, shredded
- 1 tsp. sea salt
- 2 tbsp. creamy Italian salad dressing
- ¼ tsp. white pepper
- 6 strips precooked bacon, finely shredded
- 1 bay leaf
- 1 lb. ground venison
- 4 strips precooked bacon, finely shredded
- 1 egg
- ¼ tsp. seasoned salt
- ¼ tsp. white pepper

DIRECTIONS

In a large saucepan, combine the split peas and lentils. Cover with 1 quart of water, bring to a boil and cook for 3 minutes. Remove from heat, cover and let stand for 1 hour. Drain and reserve the liquid.

Melt the butter in a large Dutch oven. Add the onion, carrot and celery and sauté until tender. Add the split peas and lentils, reserved liquid, chicken stock, potatoes, sea salt, white pepper, salad dressing and 6 strips of shredded bacon. Bring to a boil over medium heat. Add the bay leaf and reduce the heat to low. Simmer until split peas and lentils are tender, about 40 minutes.

In a medium bowl, combine the 4 strips of shredded bacon, egg, seasoned salt and white pepper. Form into teaspoon-sized dumplings and add to the simmering soup. Simmer 15 to 20 minutes or until dumplings are cooked through.

TEXICAN VENISON CHILI

SERVES 6-8

INGREDIENTS

- 2 lbs. ground venison
- 4 tbsp. olive oil
- 2 tsp. salt
- ½ cup mild chili powder
- ½ cup brown sugar
- 4 tbsp. minced garlic
- ½ cup ketchup
- 1 large red onion, diced
- 1 large white onion, diced
- 1 large can blended vegetable tomato juice
- 4 15-oz. cans Mexican-style chili beans
- 4 15-oz. cans stewed tomatoes
- 2 4-oz. cans mushroom stems and pieces
- 1 8-oz. can sliced black olives

DIRECTIONS

In a large stockpot, heat the oil and brown the venison and garlic. Add the brown sugar, chili powder, and tomato juice; simmer for 10 minutes stirring occasionally. Stir in the balance of ingredients. Reduce the heat to low and simmer for 1 hour stirring frequently.

Cool the chili and refrigerate overnight.

Reheat the next day and serve with crackers and beer.

ALWAYS BETTER THE SECOND DAY. IF YOU LIKE MORE HEAT, USE A SPICY CHILI POWDER AND ADD CHILI PEPPERS.

VENISON NOODLE SOUP

SERVES 4-6

INGREDIENTS

- 4 cups chicken stock
- 1 cup ground venison
- 2 pkgs. ramen noodles (discard the seasoning pkg)
- 1 cup bean sprouts
- 3 garlic cloves, finely minced
- 2 tbsp. teriyaki sauce
- 2 tbsp. fish sauce
- 2 tbsp. oyster sauce
- 2 large lettuce leaves, shredded
- 2 green onions, finely sliced
- 1 tbsp. fresh coriander leaves, shredded
- 1½ tsp. sriracha sauce
- 1 tbsp. brown sugar
- ½ lb. venison roast, cooked and thinly sliced

DIRECTIONS

In a large saucepan, heat the chicken stock until boiling. Add the ground venison and stir to break up the venison. Simmer for 3 to 4 minutes. Cut the ramen noodles into 4 sections each, add to the stock and simmer until tender, 6 to 8 minutes. Stir in the remaining ingredients. Simmer 3 to 5 minutes.

VENISON SPEAKEASY STEW

SERVES 6-8

INGREDIENTS

- **3 lbs. venison, cut into 2" pieces**
- **½ cup flour, mixed with ¼ teaspoon garlic salt and ¼ teaspoon pepper**
- **¼ cup olive oil**
- **3 large onions, sliced and chopped**
- **6 cloves garlic, minced**
- **½ lb. thick-cut bacon, chopped**
- **1½ tsp. curry powder**
- **1 can cream of celery soup**
- **1 can tomato soup**
- **12 oz. beer**
- **3 cups water**
- **¼ cup bourbon**

DIRECTIONS

Dredge the venison in the seasoned flour.

In a large Dutch oven, heat the olive oil over medium heat. Add the venison and brown on all sides. Stir in the onion, garlic, bacon and curry powder. Reduce heat to low and sauté, stirring constantly for 10 minutes.

In a large bowl, mix together the soups, beer, water and bourbon. Pour over the venison and mix well. Cover and simmer over low heat for 1 hour, or until venison is fork tender.

THIS STEW CAN BE SERVED OVER RICE, STEAMED POTATOES OR TOASTED BREAD. AND, OF COURSE, IT ALWAYS NEEDS A PINT NEARBY.

CREAM OF SALMON SOUP

SERVES 4

INGREDIENTS

- 1½ cups cooked salmon, flaked
- 4 cups fish stock or 1 cup of water and 3 cups chicken stock
- 2 cans condensed cream of mushroom soup
- ½ cup heavy cream
- 1 small package frozen mixed vegetables
- minced parsley

DIRECTIONS

Combine fish stock and condensed soup. Heat and stir constantly until smooth. Add the salmon and frozen vegetables. Simmer for 5 minutes, stirring occasionally, or until vegetables are hot. Remove from heat and stir in cream. Garnish with parsley.

FOR A COMPLETELY DIFFERENT FLAVOR, USE CREAM OF CELERY OR CREAM OF TOMATO SOUP.

HENRY'S BOUILLABAISSE

SERVES 6

INGREDIENTS

- **12 oz. boneless, skinless catfish fillets, cut into 1½" pieces**
- **12 oz. boneless, skinless salmon fillets, cut into 1½" pieces**
- **12 oz. crayfish tails, cooked and peeled**
- **4 oz. spicy chorizo sausage, thinly sliced**
- **¼ cup olive oil**
- **2 tbsp. butter**
- **1 medium onion, peeled, quartered and thinly sliced**
- **2 medium carrots, peeled and thinly sliced**
- **1 fennel bulb, trimmed of any yellow or brown outside stalks, cut in half and thinly sliced (reserve fronds for garnish)**
- **1 15-oz. can stewed tomatoes, chopped**
- **1 medium zucchini, quartered and sliced**
- **5 cups low sodium chicken stock**

DIRECTIONS

In a 4-quart stockpot, heat the oil. Add the onion, fennel and carrots. Reduce heat to medium and cook until the carrots are tender. Add the butter and stir in the zucchini, tomatoes and chicken stock. Bring to a boil, reduce heat to medium and add the catfish, salmon, crayfish and chorizo sausage. Cover and simmer 10 to 15 minutes or until the fish is cooked.

Serve over steamed rice and garnish with chopped fennel fronds.

IF YOU DON'T CARE FOR AN ANISE FLAVOR, SUBSTITUTE CELERY FOR THE FENNEL AND USE CHOPPED PARSLEY FOR A GARNISH.

HOT CHILI

SERVES 4-6

INGREDIENTS

- 1 lb. venison, cut into ½"–¾" cubes
- 2 tbsp. olive oil
- 2 cups chicken stock
- 1 medium onion, peeled, sliced and chopped
- 3–4 jalapeño peppers, seeded and cut into thin strips
- 1 green bell pepper, seeded and chopped
- 1 red bell pepper, seeded and chopped
- ⅛ tsp. oregano
- 1 tsp. minced garlic
- ½ tsp. granulated garlic
- ½ tsp. salt
- 1 can tomato purée
- 2 tsp. brown sugar

DIRECTIONS

In a heavy Dutch oven, heat the olive oil over medium-high heat. Add the venison and brown on all sides. Add all remaining ingredients and mix well. Reduce heat to medium and simmer, uncovered, for 30 to 40 minutes, stirring occasionally. Venison should be tender.

Serve in bowls garnished with shredded cheese, chopped green onion and/or sliced black olives.

THIS CHILI IS VERY SPICY. IF YOU WISH TO SOFTEN IT UP A BIT, ADD 2 CANS OF KIDNEY BEANS, ANOTHER CAN OF TOMATO PURÉE AND ANOTHER TBSP. OF BROWN SUGAR.

ENTRÉES

VENISON WITH ZINFANDEL AND DRIED CRANBERRIES

SERVES 6-8

THIS DISH WILL CERTAINLY IMPRESS THE IN-LAWS.

INGREDIENTS

- ½ lb. bacon, cut crosswise into ½" pieces and sautéed until almost crisp
- 3 lb. venison roast, sprinkled with ¼ cup flour
- ¼ cup olive oil
- 1 tsp. minced garlic
- 4 white and 4 black peppercorns, crushed
- 1 bay leaf
- ½ tsp. Italian seasoning
- ½ tsp. thyme, crushed
- 2 medium onions, sliced and quartered
- 2 cups quartered mushrooms
- ½ cup dried cranberries
- 2 cups peeled and sliced carrots
- 2 cups sliced celery
- 1 bottle Zinfandel wine
- 3 tbsp. beef base
- 1 cup water
- 6 medium potatoes, peeled and cut into 1" dice
- Salt and pepper to taste

DIRECTIONS

Using a heavy Dutch oven, heat the olive oil. Cut the venison roast into 2 pieces. Dredge the cut ends in flour and brown on all sides. Transfer the venison to a slow cooker and add the bacon, garlic, peppercorns, bay leaf, Italian seasoning and thyme.

In a small bowl, dissolve the beef base in the water and add to the venison along with ½ bottle of the wine. Simmer for 3 to 4 hours on low heat or until the roast is tender. Remove venison and place in a pan to cool. Adjust the seasoning of the sauce with salt and pepper. Add carrots, celery, potatoes, onion, dried cranberries and remaining wine.

Increase heat to medium and cook until vegetables are tender, about 1 hour. Add the mushrooms for the last 15 minutes of cooking time.

Slice the venison roast and arrange on an ovenproof serving platter. Keep warm in a 150 degree oven.

To serve, remove venison from the oven. Arrange the vegetables around the venison and spoon sauce over all. Serve extra sauce at the table.

MEATLOAF A LA REUBEN

SERVES 8

INGREDIENTS

- 2 lbs. ground venison
- 1 cup rye bread, cut into small cubes
- 1 medium onion, peeled, sliced and minced
- 3 tbsp. sweet pickle relish
- 1 large egg, beaten
- ¼ tsp. granulated garlic
- ¼ tsp. salt
- ⅛ tsp. white pepper
- ⅓ cup thousand island dressing
- 8 oz. fresh sauerkraut, rinsed and drained
- 5 oz. shredded Swiss cheese

FOR A SHARPER RYE FLAVOR, ADD 1/4 TSP. CRUSHED CARAWAY SEEDS.

DIRECTIONS

In a food processor fitted with a metal blade, pulse chop the venison and rye bread until combined. Add the onion, relish, egg, garlic, salt and pepper and pulse chop until thoroughly mixed. Spray a 12”x16” piece of heavy-duty foil with cooking spray. Spread the venison mixture in a 10”x14” rectangle on the foil. Top with the dressing, sauerkraut and 4 ounces of the Swiss cheese.

Using the foil as an aid, create a 14” long “jelly roll” sealing the ends and side seam. Carefully transfer the roll to a sprayed 15”x10” baking pan. Bake uncovered at 325 degrees 50 to 60 minutes, or until the internal temperature reaches 160 degrees. Sprinkle top with 1 ounce of Swiss cheese and bake until cheese is melted. Let stand 10 to 15 minutes before serving.

SPICY VENISON RED BEANS AND RICE

SERVES 6-8

INGREDIENTS

- 3 tbsp. butter
- 1 lb. ground venison
- 4 scallions, chopped
- 2 celery ribs, chopped
- 1 medium onion, chopped
- 1 medium green bell pepper, seeded and chopped
- 2 garlic cloves, chopped
- 1 can kidney beans
- 1 lb. spicy Italian sausage, casing removed
- 1 large ham hock, about 1 lb.
- 3 cup chicken stock
- 1 tsp. salt
- Hot cooked rice
- Shredded cheese, your favorite

DIRECTIONS

In a 5-quart Dutch oven, melt the butter and add the ground venison, scallions, celery, onion, bell pepper and garlic. Cook over medium heat, stirring to break up meat, until vegetables are softened and meat is cooked through. Add beans, Italian sausage, ham hock and chicken stock. Bring to a boil over high heat, stirring often. Reduce heat to low and simmer, partially covered, until beans and ham are heated through, about 1 hour. Season with salt and serve with rice and shredded cheese.

RACK OF VENISON

SERVES 2-4

INGREDIENTS

- **1 8-bone rack of venison**
- **2 tbsp. lemon juice**

DRY RUB MIX

- **1 tsp. crushed oregano**
- **½ tsp. crushed marjoram**
- **¼ tsp. sea salt**
- **¼ tsp. granulated garlic**
- **¼ tsp. dried lemon peel, ground**
- **¼ tsp. dried orange peel, ground**
- **⅛ tsp. white pepper**
- **⅛ tsp. black pepper**

USE THE SAME DRY RUB ON CHICKEN OR LAMB. FOR ADDED FLAVOR, BASTE DURING BAKING WITH GARLIC BUTTER AND LEMON JUICE.

DIRECTIONS

Mix together all dry rub ingredients in a food processor. Process for 10 seconds.

Moisten the venison rack with lemon juice and dust with the dry rub. Cover and let sit for 30 minutes. Heat a gas or charcoal grill to medium-high. Cook the venison for 3 minutes on a side. Place venison in a baking dish and roast in a 350 degree oven for 15 minutes. Let the venison sit loosely covered for 10 minutes before carving.

LITHUANIAN VENISON AND KIELBASA LOAF

SERVES 6-8

INGREDIENTS

- **4 tbsp. butter**
- **1 large onion, sliced and chopped**
- **1 large green pepper, cleaned and shopped**
- **2 cloves garlic, minced**
- **1 cup rye breadcrumbs**
- **½ cup cream**
- **2 eggs**
- **2 tsp. sweet Hungarian paprika**
- **¼ tsp. white pepper**
- **1 tsp. seasoned salt**
- **2 lbs. ground venison**
- **½ lb. smoked kielbasa, sliced ¼" and cut in half**
- **1 cup sour cream**

DIRECTIONS

Preheat oven to 350 degrees. Melt butter in a large sauté pan. Add the bacon, onion, green pepper and garlic. Cook over medium heat until the onion begins to brown, 6 to 8 minutes. Remove from heat.

In a large bowl, combine the breadcrumbs, cream, eggs, paprika, pepper and seasoned salt. Add the venison, kielbasa and the bacon/onion mixture. Knead with hands until well blended.

Pack mixture into a 9"x5" loaf pan. Bake 1 hour or until center reaches 160 degrees. Remove from oven and let cool 15 minutes before unmolding. Top each slice with a dollop of sour cream.

VENISON APPLE POT PIE

SERVES 4

INGREDIENTS

- **3 cups cubed venison loin**
- **½ cup chopped onion**
- **3 tbsp. olive oil**
- **1 can condensed cream of chicken soup**
- **1 large granny smith apple, peeled, cored and cubed**
- **⅓ cup of Craisins (dehydrated cranberries)**
- **1 tbsp. lemon juice**
- **¼ tsp. black pepper**
- **Dash of salt**
- **Pastry for single crust pie**

DIRECTIONS

In a heavy skillet, heat the oil and sauté the venison until cooked through. With a slotted spoon, remove the venison and drain on paper towel. Add onions to the skilled and cook until tender, 2 to 3 minutes. Remove from heat.

In a large stainless bowl, combine the venison, onions, soup, apple, Craisins, lemon juice, salt and pepper. Spoon the mixture into a 9", deep-dish pie pan. Place pie crust over mixture and crimp and fold the edge; cut three steam vents. Bake in a preheated 425 degree oven for 30 to 35 minutes or until crust is brown and filling is bubbly.

A GREAT DISH FOR THOSE LATE FALL DINNERS, OR A WONDERFUL ADDITION TO A BUFFET.

VENISON MINCEMEAT

MAKES 2 PIES

INGREDIENTS

- 1 lb. venison, coarsely chopped
- 2 cups apples, peeled, cored and finely diced
- 2 cups apple cider
- 1 cup currants
- 1 cup golden raisins
- 1 cup Craisins
- zest of 1 lemon
- zest of 1 orange
- ⅓ cup brown sugar
- ¼ cup white sugar
- ½ tsp. salt
- ½ tsp. cinnamon
- ¼ tsp. ground cloves
- ¼ tsp. allspice
- ½ cup candied citron, finally chopped
- 1 cup brandy

DIRECTIONS

In a heavy stockpot, combine the venison, apples and cider. Bring to a boil and stir in remaining ingredients except the brandy. Reduce heat to low. Simmer for 1 hour, stirring occasionally to prevent scorching. Remove pot from heat and carefully stir in the brandy.

DRY AGED VENISON BACKSTRAP

SERVES 6–8

INGREDIENTS

- **1–1½ lb. venison backstrap**
- **¼ cup olive oil**
- **3 tbsp. balsamic vinegar**
- **1 tbsp. fresh rosemary leaves, minced**
- **1 tsp. sea salt**
- **1 tbsp. olive oil**

DIRECTIONS

Begin the dry aging process by placing the backstrap on a rack over a shallow pan. Refrigerate 48 hours.

Preheat oven to 400 degrees. Coat the backstrap with a mixture of ¼ cup olive oil, balsamic vinegar, rosemary and sea salt. Preheat a cast iron skillet to hot and add 1 tbsp. of olive oil. Sear the backstrap on all sides for a total of 4 minutes.

Place the backstrap on a baking sheet with a rack. Bake until internal temperature reaches 130 degrees.

Remove the meat from the oven and place on a cutting board. Tent with foil and let rest for 5 to 10 minutes.

Slice ¼" thick medallions and serve with Béarnaise sauce and cranberry relish.

BREADED VENISON CHOPS

SERVES 4

INGREDIENTS

- **8 venison chops (allow at least 2 chops per person)**
- **2 large eggs**
- **3 tbsp. milk**
- **½ cup vegetable oil**

BREADING MIX

- **1 cup breadcrumbs**
- **¼ cup grated Parmesan cheese**
- **2 tsp. Italian seasoning, crushed**
- **½ tsp. granulated garlic (optional)**

THIS BREADING MIXTURE ALSO WORKS VERY WELL WITH PORK AND CHICKEN.

DIRECTIONS

Combine all breading mix ingredients. Place breading mix on a cookie sheet. In a medium bowl, whisk together the eggs and milk. Dip chops in the egg mixture and allow excess to drip off. Place the chops in the breading mix and coat both sides.

Heat a large skillet over medium-high heat. Add vegetable oil. Carefully place chops in the hot oil and turn after 1½ to 2 minutes. Chops should be nicely browned. Remove chops to baking pan. Place in a preheated 300 degree oven for 10 to 15 minutes. Serve with steamed vegetables and mashed potatoes.

ROAST VENISON WITH APRICOTS, PRUNES AND PEARS

SERVES 8

INGREDIENTS

- 3–4 lbs. boneless venison roast
- 16 dried apricots and 16 prunes, rehydrated in 2 cups cream sherry (allow at least 2 days)
- 6 strips bacon
- 4 ripe pears, cored and cut in half

SPICE RUB

- ¼ cup smoked paprika
- 1 tsp. granulated garlic
- ½ tsp. white pepper
- 1 package onion soup mix
- Mix together all spice rub ingredients in a small bowl.

BASTING SAUCE

- ¼ lb. butter
- 2 tbsp. minced garlic
- ½ cup honey
- ½ cup teriyaki sauce
- 2 cups white zinfandel wine
- 2 cups cranberry juice
- ½ tbsp. crushed dried tarragon

ADD A TEASPOON OF HOT SAUCE OR A FEW DROPS OF TABASCO TO SPARK UP THE SAUCE.

DIRECTIONS

Melt butter in a large saucepan over medium heat. Add the garlic, tarragon, honey and teriyaki sauce. Bring to a boil and stir in the wine and cranberry juice. Reduce heat to low and simmer 5 minutes. Allow to cool.

Preheat oven to 325 degrees.

Butterfly cut the roast. Lay cut side up and line the inside with bacon strips. Arrange the apricots and prunes in the center and fold over the sides to create a cylinder. Secure with kitchen twine. Dust the outside of the roast with the spice rub.

Place 5 whole carrots in the bottom of a large Dutch oven and set the venison roast on the "carrot rack."

In a large skillet, heat 2 tablespoons vegetable oil over medium-high heat. Place the pears, cut side down, in the skillet and cook for 5 to 6 minutes. Place the pears around the venison in the Dutch oven. Brush the roast and the pears with the basting sauce. Place the Dutch oven in the oven, covered, and bake 50 to 60 minutes until the internal temperature of the roast reaches 145 degrees. Baste twice during baking.

Transfer the roast to a holding tray and let stand 10 to 15 minutes. Slice the venison 1" thick and place the slices on a warm platter, arrange the pears around the roast. Drizzle warm basting sauce over the roast and serve more at the table.

VENISON AND BRAN MEATLOAF

SERVES 4-6

INGREDIENTS

- **1½ cup bran flakes, crushed**
- **2 eggs**
- **1 cup tomato salsa**
- **1 medium onion, chopped**
- **1 medium green bell pepper, chopped**
- **2 cups corn, fresh or frozen (thawed)**
- **1½ tsp. garlic salt**
- **¼ tsp. pepper**
- **2 lbs. ground venison**
- **½ lb. thick sliced bacon, finely chopped**
- **⅓ cup ketchup**

DIRECTIONS

Preheat oven to 350 degrees. In a large bowl, mix corn flakes, eggs, salsa, onion and bell pepper with a fork. Add venison and bacon and knead with your hands until fully blended. Transfer to an 8"x4" loaf pan.

Bake until center reaches 160 degrees, about 1 hour. Let stand 5 minutes before slicing. During last 15 minutes of baking, spread ketchup over top of the loaf.

VENISON AND NOODLE CASSEROLE

SERVES 6-8

INGREDIENTS

- ¼ lb. bacon, chopped
- 2 lbs. ground venison
- 1 large onion, sliced and chopped
- 2 cloves garlic, minced
- 4 oz. mozzarella cheese, shredded
- 6 oz. ricotta cheese
- 2 eggs, beaten
- 2 cans tomato soup
- 3 tbsp. A-1 Sauce
- 3 tbsp. brown sugar
- salt and pepper to taste
- 6 oz. wide egg noodles, cooked according to package directions
- 4 oz. grated Parmesan, grated

DIRECTIONS

In a large skillet, brown bacon until crisp. Remove the bacon from the skillet and reserve for later use. Add venison to bacon fat and brown. Stir in the onion and garlic and cook over medium heat until onion is tender.

In a medium bowl, mix together the ricotta, mozzarella, eggs, soup, A-1 Sauce and brown sugar. Season with salt and pepper to taste.

Using a 9"x13" baking dish, layer ½ lb of the venison, ⅓ of the noodles and ⅓ of the sauce. Continue layering and top with grated Parmesan cheese.

Bake in a preheated 325 degree oven for 20 to 30 minutes. Let stand 15 minutes before serving. Serve with a green salad.

VENISON AND POTATO BURGERS

SERVES 6–8

INGREDIENTS

- **1 lb. venison, cut in 1" cubes**
- **1 lb. pork shoulder, cut in 1" cubes**
- **6 strips precooked bacon, cut in ½" pieces**
- **½ lb. Yukon gold potatoes, boiled and cut in 1" cubes**
- **1 large egg, beaten**
- **1 tbsp. butter**
- **2 tbsp. olive oil**

SPICE BLEND

- **¼ tsp. white pepper**
- **¼ tsp. dried sage**
- **¼ tsp. dried basil**
- **1 tsp. salt**
- **2 tbsp. brown sugar**
- **½ tsp. smoked paprika**

DIRECTIONS

In a large bowl, combine the venison, pork, bacon and potatoes. In a small bowl, combine the spice blend ingredients and mix well. Distribute the spice blend over the meat mixture. Cover and refrigerate at least 1 hour. Remove the meat mixture from the refrigerator. Grind or chop meat mixture to a uniform consistency similar to ground beef. Add the egg and knead with hands to completely incorporate

Divide mixture into 8-ounce portions. Form into burger patties. Using a nonstick skillet, melt the butter and olive oil over medium heat. Brown the burgers 3 to 4 minutes on each side.

VENISON AND POTATO CHOWDER

SERVES 6–8

INGREDIENTS

- 1 lb. ground venison
- 6 strips precooked bacon, chopped
- 1 medium white onion, chopped
- 2 celery stalks, sliced
- 1 large red bell pepper, diced
- 2 cup chicken stock
- 2 medium Yukon gold potatoes, cut into ½" cubes
- 1 bay leaf
- 1 tsp. marjoram
- ½ tsp. salt
- ¼ tsp. white pepper
- 1 cup heavy cream

DIRECTIONS

In a large saucepan or Dutch oven, cook the venison, onion, celery and green pepper for 5 to 8 minutes. Stir occasionally to break up the venison. Add the precooked bacon for the last 3 minutes of cooking. Add chicken stock, potato, bay leaf, marjoram, salt and white pepper. Simmer until potatoes are tender. Stir in heavy cream and heat through.

SIMMERED VENISON

SERVES 6-8

INGREDIENTS

- **2-3 lbs. boneless venison shoulder or leg**
- **2 large onions, sliced**
- **3 large carrots, sliced**
- **1 tsp. seasoned salt**
- **3 cups chicken stock**

DIRECTIONS

Place the venison in a large Dutch oven. Add the onions, carrots and seasoned salt. Pour in the chicken stock. Cover and cook at a simmer for 1 hour for each pound of meat. Meat should be tender but not stringy.

Remove from heat and allow meat to cool in the broth. Remove the onions and carrots. Transfer the venison to a bowl and cover with plastic wrap. Refrigerate and slice as needed for sandwich meat or an addition to a dinner salad.

HUNGARIAN VENISON PAPRIKASH

SERVES 4-6

INGREDIENTS

- 2 lbs. venison steak, cut into bite-size pieces
- 1 medium onion, thinly sliced
- 1 medium green pepper, cut into ¼" strips
- 1 15-oz. can stewed tomatoes
- 2 tbsp. Hungarian sweet paprika
- ½ cup chicken broth
- 1 tbsp. flour
- ¾ cup sour cream
- Olive oil

DIRECTIONS

In a large nonstick skillet over medium-high heat, cook the venison in 1 tablespoon olive oil until lightly browned on all sides.

Reduce heat to medium and add the onion pepper and paprika to the skillet. Cook and stir until the onion is soft. Sprinkle flour over the venison/vegetable mixture and stir for 1 minute. Add the tomatoes and chicken stock and cook 3 to 4 minutes, or until the sauce is slightly thickened. Slowly stir in the sour cream and heat for 1 to 2 minutes. Adjust seasoning as desired. Serve over buttered noodles.

AS A VARIATION, ADD COOKED DICED POTATOES, CARROTS AND PEAS WHEN YOU ADD THE SOUR CREAM.

CAROLINA BBQ

SERVES 10-12

INGREDIENTS

- 4–5 lb. venison shoulder roast
- 1 large onion, peeled, sliced and chopped
- 4 stalks celery, sliced
- 2 carrots, peeled and sliced
- 8 peppercorns
- 2 cups red wine
- 2 cups chicken stock
- 2 bay leaves

TRADITIONALLY, THESE SANDWICHES ARE SERVED TOPPED WITH COLESLAW.

BBQ SAUCE

- 1 medium onion, peeled, sliced and chopped
- 1 tsp. minced garlic
- 2 tbsp. butter
- 2 cups prepared yellow mustard
- 1½ cup brown sugar
- 1½ cup cider vinegar
- 4 tbsp. chili powder
- 2 tsp. black pepper
- 2 tsp. white pepper
- ½ tsp. cayenne pepper
- 1 cup teriyaki sauce

DIRECTIONS

Place the venison and vegetables in a large slow cooker. Add peppercorns, bay leaves, wine, chicken stock and water to cover. Cook on low heat 6 to 8 hours or until venison is very tender. Remove venison to a tray and allow to cool until it can be shredded by hand. Place in a large bowl. If you'd like, save the stock for later use in soups or sauces.

Keep the shredded pork warm if you plan to serve it immediately or cool in the refrigerator for later use.

To prepare the BBQ sauce, melt the butter over medium heat in a 3–4 quart Dutch oven. Sauté the onion until opaque. Stir in the garlic and cook 1 to 2 minutes. Reduce the heat to low and stir in the remaining sauce ingredients. Cook 5 minutes, stirring often. Remove sauce from the heat. Add 2 cups to the venison and mix well. Serve on fresh kaiser rolls with additional sauce on the side.

MARSH-STYLE VENISON LOAF

SERVES 6

INGREDIENTS

- 2 cups chicken broth
- ½ cup wild rice
- 2 lbs. ground venison
- 3 stalks celery, finely sliced
- 2 cloves garlic, minced
- 1 medium onion, sliced and chopped
- 1 medium carrot, shredded
- 2 eggs
- ½ cup cream
- ½ cup Craisins, soaked in red wine 1 hour
- ½ cup seasoned breadcrumbs
- 8 slices precooked bacon, chopped
- ¼ cup fresh parsley, chopped
- ½ tsp. basil
- ½ tsp. oregano
- 1 tsp. salt
- ¼ tsp. white pepper
- currant jelly (optional)

DIRECTIONS

In a medium saucepan, bring the chicken broth to a boil. Stir in the wild rice, reduce heat to low and cover. Simmer until the rice "blooms" and is tender, 50 to 60 minutes. Drain liquid from rice.

Preheat oven to 350 degrees. In a large bowl, combine rice and venison with the remaining ingredients. Knead with hands until well blended. Pack into a buttered 9"x5" loaf pan.

Bake until center reaches 160 degrees. Remove from oven and let stand 10 minutes before removing from pan and slicing. Serve with currant jelly.

QUICK VENISON AND SHRIMP GUMBO

SERVES 6-8

INGREDIENTS

- 1 tbsp. olive oil
- 1 lb. ground venison
- 3 tbsp. butter
- 2 tbsp. flour
- ½ tsp. crushed thyme
- ½ tsp. crushed basil
- ½ tsp. salt
- ¼ tsp. crushed red pepper or Cajun seasoning
- 4 cups beef broth
- ½ lb. andouille or other smoked sausage, sliced ½" thick
- 2 15-oz. cans stewed tomatoes, chopped
- 3 tbsp. white rice
- 1 pkg. frozen okra, thawed
- 1 lb. fresh shrimp (26–30), peeled and deveined
- cooked rice
- hot sauce

DIRECTIONS

In a 5 to 6 quart Dutch oven, heat the oil and brown the venison. In a separate saucepan, melt the butter. Stir in the flour, thyme, basil, salt and red pepper or Cajun seasoning. Slowly mix in the beef broth until blended.

Stir the mixture into the venison. Add the sausage and tomatoes, rice and okra. Reduce heat to low and simmer for 20 minutes or until rice is tender. Stir in the shrimp and cook until they are pink. Serve over cooked rice and season with hot sauce as desired.

VENISON WITH BEER AND DILL

SERVES 6–8

INGREDIENTS

- **2–3 lb. venison roast**
- **1 tbsp. olive oil**
- **3 tbsp. flour**
- **¼ tsp. salt**
- **¼ tsp. pepper**
- **3 tbsp. olive oil**
- **3 medium onions, minced**
- **2 cloves garlic, minced**
- **2 cups dark beer**
- **1 tsp. brown sugar**
- **1 tsp. seasoned salt**
- **6 carrots**
- **2 tbsp. fresh dill, chopped**

DIRECTIONS

Rub the roast with 1 tbsp. olive oil and season with salt and pepper. Dust with flour.

Heat 3 tbsp. olive oil in a large skillet over medium heat. Brown the roast on all sides. Transfer the roast to a bowl. Brown the onion and garlic in the skillet on medium heat, about 3 minutes. Stir in the beer, brown sugar and seasoned salt.

Arrange the carrots in the bottom of a Dutch oven. Place the roast on the carrots, add the beer mixture. Cover and reduce heat to low. Cook for 2 hours. Transfer the roast to a warm plate and let rest for at least 15 minutes. Remove the carrots and strain the cooking liquid. Return liquid to Dutch oven, bring to a boil and cook until thickened.

Slice and garnish with chopped dill and the thickened sauce. Serve with potatoes and a green vegetable.

BARBECUED VENISON RIBS

SERVES 6–8

INGREDIENTS

- 3–5 lbs venison ribs, trimmed of fat and cut into serving pieces
- olive oil
- salt & pepper

SAUCE

- 1 large can frozen orange juice concentrate
- 1 cup water
- ¼ cup teriyaki sauce
- 2 tbsp. brown sugar
- ¼ cup lemon juice
- 1 tsp. dry mustard
- 1 tbsp. minced garlic
- 1 cup ketchup
- 3 tbsp. Worcestershire sauce
- 1 medium onion, minced
- ¼ cup sorghum molasses
- 3 tbsp. chili powder

DIRECTIONS

Preheat oven to 425 degrees. Rub ribs with olive oil and season with salt and pepper. Place ribs flat in a roasting pan (do not overlap). Bake 25 minutes, turn and bake another 20 minutes or until browned.

While ribs are baking, prepare the sauce. In a large saucepan over low heat, combine the water and orange juice concentrate. Add the remaining sauce ingredients. Simmer for 20 minutes, remove from heat.

Reduce oven temperature to 250 degrees. Baste ribs with sauce every 20 minutes for 3 to 4 hours or until fork tender.

BARBECUED VENISON TENDERLOIN

SERVES 4-6

INGREDIENTS

- 2 whole venison tenderloins
- 2 oz. Grand Marnier liqueur
- ¼ lb. sweet butter
- 2 shallots, finely minced
- 1 clove garlic, minced
- ¼ tsp. oregano
- ¼ tsp. cumin
- ¼ tsp. salt
- 2 tbsp. chili powder
- 2 cups ketchup
- ¼ cup molasses
- ¼ cup red wine vinegar
- 1 cup orange juice

THIS SAUCE IS CITRUS-BASED WITH ORANGE FLAVORS; TRY LEMON, LIME OR APRICOT, BUT CHANGE THE LIQUEUR TO AN APPROPRIATE FLAVOR.

DIRECTIONS

Barbecue Sauce:

In a 3-quart saucepan, melt the butter over medium heat. Add the shallots and garlic and sauté until the shallots are translucent. Add the dry spices and continue cooking for 2 to 3 minutes, stirring constantly. Add the ketchup, molasses, vinegar, orange juice and Grand Marnier; mix thoroughly. Reduce heat, cover and simmer for 1 hour. Store finished sauce in a covered container under refrigeration.

Barbecued Tenderloin:

Place the venison tenderloins on a sheet of buttered heavy-duty foil. Cover the tenderloins with 1 cup of barbecue sauce. Fold over the foil and seal. Place the foil package on a hot outdoor grill for 20 to 30 minutes or place in a preheated 350 degree oven for 40 minutes. Remove package from heat and let sit 15 minutes before slicing. Serve with fresh vegetables and steamed new potatoes.

VENISON STROGANOFF

SERVES 6-8

INGREDIENTS

- 1½ lbs. ground venison
- ½ lb. ground pork
- 1 egg, lightly beaten
- ½ tsp. white pepper
- ¼ cup Parmesan cheese, grated
- ¼ tsp. nutmeg
- ½ tsp. salt
- 2 tbsp. butter
- 1 medium onion, minced
- 1 tsp. garlic, minced
- 1 can cream of mushroom soup
- 1 small can mushrooms, sliced
- 3 tbsp. ketchup
- 1 tbsp. Worcestershire sauce
- 1 cup sour cream
- ¼ cup sherry

DIRECTIONS

Mix the venison, pork, egg, pepper, Parmesan cheese, nutmeg and salt in a medium bowl. Divide into 8 equal portions and form into thick patties.

In a large skillet brown the patties in the butter and remove to a covered plate. Add the onion and garlic to the skillet and sauté for 3 minutes.

Add the mushroom soup, mushrooms, ketchup, Worcestershire sauce, sour cream and sherry. Mix well. Place the venison patties back into the skillet. Cover and cook over low heat 15 to 20 minutes. Do not allow to boil.

Serve over buttered egg noodles.

VENISON STUFFED GREEN PEPPERS

SERVES 6

INGREDIENTS

- ½ lb. ground venison
- ½ lb. bulk sweet Italian sausage
- ½ lb. bulk mild Italian sausage
- 1 medium onion, peeled, sliced and chopped
- ½ cup cooked wild rice
- ½ cup ricotta cheese
- 6 green bell peppers, tops, seeds and white membrane removed
- 1 18 oz.-can Italian vegetable soup
- 1 cup chicken stock
- 6 slices mozzarella cheese

DIRECTIONS

Preheat oven to 325 degrees. Coat a deep covered Dutch oven with nonstick spray.

In a medium bowl, mix the venison, sausages, onion, wild rice and ricotta cheese. Stuff each pepper with an equal portion of this mixture and arrange them in the Dutch oven.

Pour the soup and the chicken stock over the peppers and top each with a slice of mozzarella. Bake for 40 to 50 minutes or until internal temperature reaches 160 degrees.

THIS IS THE PERFECT DISH
FOR A CASUAL BUFFET DINNER.

VENISON GRAVY AND BISCUITS

SERVES 4-6

INGREDIENTS

- **2 lbs. ground venison**
- **¼ lb. unsalted butter**
- **½ tsp. granulated garlic**
- **½ tsp. salt**
- **¼ tsp. white pepper**
- **¼ cup flour**
- **2 cups heavy cream**
- **1 can prepared biscuits, baked according to manufacturer's instructions**

DIRECTIONS

In a large sauté pan, melt the butter and brown the venison. Reduce the heat, add garlic, salt and pepper, and stir in the flour.

Slowly add the cream, stirring constantly. If mixture is too thick, add a small amount of additional cream.

To serve, split a hot biscuit and spoon over a generous portion of gravy.

LEFTOVER VENISON MEATLOAF AND POTATO PIE

SERVES 6-8

INGREDIENTS

- **1 4.2 oz. carton dehydrated hash brown potatoes**
- **4 eggs, beaten**
- **2 cups leftover venison meatloaf, crumbled**
- **¾ cup sharp cheddar cheese, grated**
- **4 green onions, thinly sliced**
- **½ tsp. salt**
- **½ tsp. smoked paprika**

DIRECTIONS

Preheat oven to 375 degrees. Rehydrate the hash browns according to package directions. Combine all ingredients in a large bowl and mix well.

Pack the mixture into a buttered 10" deep pie plate. Bake 30 to 40 minutes until top is golden brown and the pie is completely set. Remove from oven and let sit 10 minutes before cutting.

CHOW MEIN WITH VENISON AND SHRIMP

SERVES 6

INGREDIENTS

- **1 tsp. salt**
- **1 tablespoon cornstarch**
- **1 cup chicken stock**
- **6 tbsp. vegetable oil**
- **1 lb. venison, cut into very thin strips 2" long**
- **1 cup raw shrimp, peeled, deveined and cut in half lengthwise**
- **2 carrots, coarsely grated**
- **1 cup raw mushrooms, cut into matchsticks**
- **3 stalks celery, cut thinly on the diagonal**
- **4 scallions, sliced very thin on the diagonal**
- **4 tbsp. teriyaki sauce**
- **4–6 cups medium noodles (about 8 oz. uncooked fettuccine noodles)**

DIRECTIONS

Mix the salt and cornstarch with the chicken stock.

Set a large wok or sauté pan over high heat for 30 seconds. Add 3 tablespoons of vegetable oil and wait until it begins to smoke. Add the venison and stir-fry for 2 minutes. Add the shrimp and continue cooking for 1 minute more.

Add the carrots, mushrooms, celery, scallions and teriyaki sauce. Stir-fry for 3 minutes. Pour in the cornstarch mixture and stir until thickened. Adjust seasoning with additional salt and teriyaki if desired.

In a large skillet, heat the remaining 3 tablespoons of vegetable oil over medium heat. Add the cooked noodles and stir until heated through. Transfer noodles to a serving bowl and top with the venison/shrimp mixture.

HEAT LEFTOVERS FOR LUNCH AND SERVE ON A HAMBURGER BUN—YOUR NOT-SO-TRADITIONAL CHOW MEIN SANDWICH.

VENISON RAGOUT

SERVES 6-8

INGREDIENTS

- 3 tbsp. olive oil
- 2-3 lbs. venison, cut in 1" pieces
- ¼ lb. fresh button mushrooms
- 2 doz. pearl onions, peeled
- ½ cup beef stock
- 1 can tomato paste
- 1½ cups red wine
- ¾ cup dry sherry
- ¼ cup ruby port
- 4 tbsp. flour
- 1 small clove garlic, crushed
- ¼ tsp. black pepper
- 2 bay leaves
- egg noodles

DIRECTIONS

Heat the olive oil in a heavy Dutch oven over medium heat. Brown the venison in the olive oil. Transfer the venison to a bowl. Add the mushrooms and onions to the Dutch oven and cook until onions begin to brown. Place the mushrooms and onions in the bowl containing the browned venison.

Turn off heat and combine the beef stock and tomato paste in the Dutch oven. In a separate bowl, mix the wines with the flour to form a thin paste. Add this to the Dutch oven and set heat to medium. Stir until the liquid almost boils. Add the venison, mushrooms, onions, garlic, pepper and bay leaves. Cover and place in a 350 degree oven for 1½ to 2 hours or until venison is tender. Serve over egg noodles.

CRANBERRY VENISON POT ROAST

SERVES 6

INGREDIENTS

- 4 lb. boneless venison roast
- 4 cups cranapple juice
- 1 15-oz. can whole cranberry sauce
- 1 cup teriyaki sauce
- 1 medium onion, peeled and chopped fine
- 1 clove garlic, minced
- ¼ tsp. ground cloves

DIRECTIONS

Place the venison roast in a one-gallon storage bag that seals, and add 2 cups cranapple juice; seal and refrigerate venison for at least 4 hours or overnight.

Place the venison roast in a 5-quart slow cooker. In a small bowl, mix the cranberry sauce with 2 cups cranapple juice, garlic, onions, and ground cloves. Pour the mixture over the venison roast; if necessary, add additional cranapple juice to cover the roast. Cover and cook on low 7 to 8 hours or until the venison is tender. Serve over hot rice or buttered noodles.

BURSTING WITH FLAVOR, THIS ROAST IS SO TENDER IT CAN BE CUT WITH A FORK.

MY MOTHER'S VENISON MEATLOAF

SERVES 4-6

INGREDIENTS

- **1 medium onion, chopped**
- **2 eggs**
- **⅔ cup oatmeal**
- **½ cup ketchup**
- **1 tbsp. Worcestershire sauce**
- **1 tsp. salt**
- **¼ tsp. pepper**
- **1 lb. ground venison**
- **1 lb. bulk pork sausage**
- **3 tbsp. ketchup**

DIRECTIONS

Preheat oven to 375 degrees. In a medium bowl, combine the onion, eggs, oatmeal, ½ cup ketchup, Worcestershire sauce, salt and pepper. Add the venison and pork sausage, and blend well.

Place mixture in an 8"x4" loaf pan. Place on a baking sheet and bake, uncovered, for 45 minutes. Spread the remaining 3 tablespoons of ketchup over the top of the meatloaf and bake until a meat thermometer in the center of the loaf reads 160 degrees, approximately 15 minutes longer. Remove from the oven and let stand for 5 minutes before slicing.

MY MOTHER WOULD CALL THIS HER "DEPRESSION MEATLOAF."

SOUTH OF THE BORDER VENISON AND RICE

SERVES 6-8

INGREDIENTS

- **1½ lbs. venison, trimmed of fat and cut into ½" cubes.**
- **3 tbsp. unsalted butter**
- **3 10-oz. cans stewed tomatoes**
- **1 serano chili, seeded and chopped**
- **1 tsp. chili powder**
- **½ tsp. salt**
- **1 tbsp. brown sugar**
- **1 cup rice**

DIRECTIONS

In a Dutch oven over high heat, brown the venison cubes in the butter. Lower heat to medium and simmer until tender.

Drain the tomatoes, reserving the liquid. Add water to equal 2 cups. Mix the chili powder, salt and brown sugar with the liquid. Add tomatoes, chili, rice and the seasoned liquid to the venison. Bring to a boil. Lower heat to medium, cover and simmer until rice is tender and the liquid is absorbed. Serve with a steamed vegetable.

CORIANDER AND HONEY GLAZED VENISON CHOPS

SERVES 6-8

INGREDIENTS

- **6–8 boneless venison chops, cut 1½" thick**
- **2 tbsp. olive oil**
- **1 tbsp. ground coriander**
- **2 tbsp. Dijon mustard**
- **½ tsp. smoked paprika**
- **3 tbsp. honey**
- **2 tbsp. lime juice**
- **¼ cup teriyaki**

DIRECTIONS

Preheat oven to 400 degrees.

In a small bowl, mix together the coriander, mustard, paprika, honey, lime juice and teriyaki sauce.

In an ovenproof frying pan, heat the oil and sear the chops for 1½ to 2 minutes on each side. Apply coriander and honey glaze to both sides of the chops and place pan in the preheated oven for 8 to 10 minutes (chops will be rare to medium rare).

THE CORIANDER HONEY GLAZE CAN BE USED ON STEAMED CARROTS OR WINTER SQUASH.

SOUTHWESTERN VENISON MEATLOAF

SERVES 4-6

INGREDIENTS

- 1 cup tomato salsa, drained
- 1 cup tortilla chips, finely crushed
- 1 egg
- 1 small onion, chopped
- 1 garlic clove, minced
- 1 small fresh green chili, seeded and minced
- 1 tbsp. chili powder (medium heat)
- 1 tsp. celery salt
- ½ tsp. ground cumin
- 2 lbs. ground venison
- ½ cup sharp cheddar cheese, shredded
- ½ lb. thick sliced bacon, diced

DIRECTIONS

Preheat oven to 375 degrees. In a medium bowl, combine salsa, tortilla chips, egg, onion, garlic, chili, chili powder, celery salt and cumin. Mix well.

Add the venison and bacon, knead with your hands until fully blended. Pack mixture into an 8"x4" loaf pan. Place on a baking sheet and bake, uncovered, until center reaches 165 degrees, about 1 hour. Sprinkle shredded cheese on top of loaf and bake about 3 additional minutes, or until cheese melts. Let stand 5 minutes before slicing.

VENISON AND VEGETABLE CASSEROLE

SERVES 6-8

INGREDIENTS

- **3 tbsp. peanut oil**
- **2 lbs. ground venison**
- **2 large onions, sliced and chopped**
- **4 stalks celery, chopped**
- **2 cans cream of celery soup**
- **milk**
- **6 cups hash brown potatoes**
- **6 medium carrots, peeled and sliced**
- **¼ cup Parmesan cheese, grated**

DIRECTIONS

Heat the oil over medium-high heat in a Dutch oven. Brown the venison. Add the onion and celery and cook until the vegetables are tender. Place the soup in a 4-cup measure and stir in milk until there is 3 cups.

Butter a 9"x13" baking dish. Layer ⅓ of the hash browns, ⅓ of the venison, ⅓ of the carrots and ⅓ of the soup mixture. Continue layering and top with the grated Parmesan.

Bake in a preheated 325 degree oven for 1 hour or until carrots and potatoes are tender.

VENISON AND WILD RICE CASSEROLE

SERVES 6-8

INGREDIENTS

- 2 lbs. venison steak, cut in ½" cubes
- ½ cup flour seasoned with ¼ tsp salt and ¼ tsp. pepper
- ⅓ cup olive oil
- 8 strips precooked bacon, cut in ½" pieces
- 1 cup fresh mushrooms, sliced
- 1 cup celery, sliced
- ½ cup onion, minced
- ½ cup Craisins
- ¼ tsp. celery salt
- ¼ tsp. granulated garlic
- ¼ tsp. black pepper
- ½ tbsp. dehydrated onion
- 1 tsp. sweet paprika
- 3 cups cooked wild rice
- 1 can cream of mushroom soup
- 3 large eggs, beaten
- 1 cup white cheddar cheese, shredded

DIRECTIONS

Dust the venison with the seasoned flour. Heat the olive oil in a large sauté pan over medium heat. Brown the venison in the olive oil. Transfer the venison to a large bowl. Add the bacon, mushrooms, celery, onion and Craisins to the Dutch oven. Sauté and stir until onions are wilted.

Stir in the celery salt, granulated garlic, black pepper, dehydrated onion, sweet paprika and soup. Add to the bowl with the venison. Stir in the wild rice and fold in the beaten eggs. Place in a buttered baking dish. Top with cheese and bake at 350 degrees 1 to 1 ½ hours. Let set for 10 minutes after you remove the casserole from the oven.

VENISON MEATBALL CASSEROLE WITH APPLES AND SAUERKRAUT

SERVES 6-8

INGREDIENTS

- 2 lbs. ground venison
- ½ cup minced onion
- 2 slices white bread soaked in white wine
- 1 egg, beaten
- 1 tsp. salt
- ⅛ tsp. pepper
- 2 cups sauerkraut, rinsed and drained
- 6 precooked bacon strips, roughly chopped
- 3 large apples, cored and sliced ¼" thick
- 2 tbsp. brown sugar
- ½ cup apple juice
- ½ cup white wine from the soaked bread

DIRECTIONS

In a large bowl, combine the venison and onion. Squeeze the wine from the bread, saving the wine. Break the bread into small pieces and add to the venison. Add the salt and pepper to the beaten egg and whisk. Add the egg to the venison, mixing thoroughly. Form into medium-sized meatballs.

Place the meatballs on an oiled baking sheet. Bake in a preheated 325 degree oven for 45 minutes.

Using a greased 9"x13" baking dish, layer the ingredients as follows:
Sauerkraut
Bacon and apples
Meatballs and brown sugar

Add the apple juice to the reserved white wine to make one cup and pour over the casserole. Cover with foil and bake in a preheated 325 degree oven for 1 hour.

STEAK AU POIVRE

SERVES 6

THE DIJON CREAM SAUCE WILL ENHANCE ANY WILD OR DOMESTIC RED OR WHITE MEAT. FOR AN ADDED PUNCH, USE COGNAC INSTEAD OF BRANDY.

INGREDIENTS

- 3 lbs. venison, short loin or strip loin, cut into 8 oz. steaks at least 1" thick and tenderized with a spring loaded multi-blade meat tenderizer or textured meat mallet
- 4 tbsp. white and black peppercorns, coarsely ground or crushed
- Dijon mustard
- 1 tbsp. olive oil

DIJON CREAM SAUCE

- ½ cup minced shallots
- 1 clove garlic, minced
- 1 cup beef stock, mixed with
- 1 tbsp. Knorr Demi-Glace Sauce Mix
- 2 tbsp. butter
- 1 tbsp. Dijon mustard
- ¼ cup brandy

DIRECTIONS

Spread a thin layer of Dijon mustard on each side of the steak, press into the peppercorns to coat.

Heat a heavy, seasoned skillet to a level where a drop of water bounces on the surface. Add the olive oil and brown the steaks 2 minutes on each side. Reduce heat and cook to desired degree of doneness.

Melt the butter in a 2-quart saucepan and gently sauté the shallot and garlic over low heat until translucent. Whisk in the mustard, beef stock and brandy. Continue stirring until the sauce has thickened.

To serve, plate the steaks and spoon the sauce over.

VENISON MEATLOAF WITH PAN GRAVY

SERVES 6-8

INGREDIENTS

- **1 large onion, finely chopped**
- **1 large green bell pepper, finely chopped**
- **2 large eggs**
- **¾ cup rolled oats**
- **½ cup tomato sauce**
- **2 tbsp. steak sauce**
- **¾ tsp. garlic salt**
- **½ tsp. pepper**
- **2 lbs. ground venison**
- **1 lb. bulk pork sausage**
- **3 tbsp. butter**
- **1 tbsp. flour**
- **2 cups chicken stock**
- **1 beef bouillon cube**
- **2 cups milk or cream**

DIRECTIONS

Preheat oven to 375 degrees. In a medium bowl, combine the onion, bell pepper, egg, oats, tomato sauce, steak sauce, garlic salt and ¼ tsp. pepper. Mix well. Add the ground meats and blend well.

Line an 8" x 4" loaf pan with plastic wrap. Pack the meatloaf mixture into the pan. Invert the pan and unmold the meatloaf onto a lightly oiled baking sheet. Bake until the center reaches 165 degrees, about 1 hour. Remove from oven and let sit 5 minutes. Cover with foil to keep warm.

While the meatloaf is baking, melt the butter in a medium saucepan over medium heat. Add the flour and cook, whisking constantly until flour is lightly browned, about 2 minutes.

Whisk in the chicken stock and bouillon cube and bring to a boil, whisking until thickened and smooth. Add pan juices, reduce heat to medium-low and simmer, stirring often, for 5 minutes. Stir in the milk or cream. Season with salt and pepper to taste.

VENISON MINI MEATLOAVES BRAISED IN BROWN SUGAR AND BOURBON

SERVES 6-8

INGREDIENTS

- 2½ lbs. ground venison
- 6 slices bacon, chopped
- 1 cup seasoned breadcrumbs
- 2 eggs, beaten
- 1 10½-ounce can beef consommé
- 2 cups baby carrots, peeled
- 2 cups size B red potatoes
- 2 10¾-ounce cans stewed tomatoes
- ¼ cup brown sugar
- ¼ cup bourbon

DIRECTIONS

Mix together the venison, bacon, breadcrumbs, eggs and ½ can consommé. Transfer to a 9"x13" baking dish and shape into a log. Cut the log into 8 equal sections. Form the sections into mini loaves. Arrange in the baking dish leaving room for the vegetables.

Distribute the carrots, potatoes and stewed tomatoes in the pan. Mix together the remaining consommé, brown sugar and bourbon. Pour over the loaves and vegetables. Cover the dish with foil and bake in a preheated 350 degree oven for 30 minutes. Remove the foil and bake until the vegetables are tender.

VENISON BRATWURST

MAKES 32 BRATWURST

INGREDIENTS

- **4 lbs. venison, coarsely ground**
- **4 lbs. pork shoulder or pork butt, coarsely ground**
- **8 oz. German ale**
- **3 tbsp. Morton's Tender Quick**
- **3 tbsp. Penzey's Bratwurst Seasoning**
- **2 tsp. ground coriander**
- **2 tsp. white sugar**

DIRECTIONS

In a large bowl, combine all ingredients and mix well. Cover and refrigerate for 24 hours. Mix again and stuff natural casing forming links about 6" long. Remove any air pockets by piercing with a large needle.

Package in plastic bags, separating sausages with wax paper, and freeze for later use.

To prepare the sausage, defrost. Place in a deep skillet over high heat with 1 cup water. Bring to a boil, cover, reduce heat to low and simmer for 10 minutes. Pour off any remaining water. Add one tablespoon of oil, increase heat to medium-high and cook until sausages are browned.

YOU CAN ALSO FOREGO THE CASINGS AND FORM THE MEAT MIXTURE INTO PATTIES FOR COOKING ON THE GRILL AND SERVING ON RYE OR PRETZEL BUNS.

MUSTARD-GLAZED VENISON TENDERLOIN

SERVES 2–4

INGREDIENTS

- ¼ cup brown sugar
- 2 tbsp. butter, softened
- ¼ cup whole-grain mustard
- ¼ tsp. granulated garlic
- 1 large onion, thinly sliced
- 1 lb. venison tenderloin
- 6 fresh basil leaves

DIRECTIONS

Preheat oven to 400 degrees. In a medium bowl, combine the brown sugar, butter, mustard and granulated garlic.

Place a sheet of heavy-duty aluminum foil large enough to accommodate the venison on a flat surface. Spray the foil with cooking spray. Layer the onions down the center and place the venison on top of the onions. Coat the venison with half of the brown sugar/mustard mixture.

Bring the long edges of the foil together and double fold. Do the same on the ends. Place the packet on a baking sheet. Place in the oven. Immediately reduce heat to 350 degrees and bake for 20 to 25 minutes, or until the internal temperature reads 130 degrees.

Remove the venison from the oven and carefully open by cutting the top with a sharp knife. Heat oven to broil (400–425 degrees). Spread remaining brown sugar/mustard mixture on the venison and place in the oven for 1 to 3 minutes, or until a light crust forms on top. Remove from the oven and let rest for 10 minutes before slicing. Garnish with fresh basil leaves.

THIS RECIPE WORKS EQUALLY WELL WITH VENISON BACK STRAP.

CUBAN PULLED VENISON

SERVES 6-8

INGREDIENTS

- **2 tbsp. olive oil**
- **2 large green peppers, seeded and coarsely chopped**
- **2 medium onions, sliced and coarsely chopped**
- **3 cloves garlic, chopped**
- **1 tbsp. cumin, ground**
- **1 tbsp. oregano**
- **2 cups chicken stock**
- **1 15-oz. can stewed tomatoes, chopped**
- **4 lbs. boneless venison, large pieces**
- **4 spicy chorizo sausages**
- **1 cup pimento-stuffed olives, sliced**
- **1 tbsp. red wine vinegar**
- **8 cups white rice, cooked**

DIRECTIONS

Preheat oven to 325 degrees.

In a large heavy Dutch oven, heat the olive oil over medium heat. Sauté the peppers, onions and garlic for 8 to 10 minutes. Stir in the cumin, oregano, chicken stock and tomatoes. Heat to a simmer and add the venison and sausages. Cover and place in the oven. Bake for 3 to 4 hours or until the venison is tender.

Transfer the venison and sausage to separate bowls. Shred the venison and return to the Dutch oven. Thinly slice the sausage and return to the Dutch oven. Stir in the olives and vinegar. Serve in bowls over white rice.

GARNISH EACH SERVING WITH SLICED GREEN ONIONS AND FRESH CILANTRO, AND DON'T FORGET THAT GLASS OF PREMIUM CUBAN RUM.

VENISON AND WILD RICE QUICHE

SERVES 6-8

INGREDIENTS

- 1 9" pie shell
- 3 tbsp. butter
- 1 lb. ground venison
- 4 strips precooked bacon, crumbled
- 3 tbsp. chives, minced
- ¾ cup fresh mushrooms, sliced
- 1 cup Swiss cheese, grated
- 2 eggs
- 1 cup heavy cream
- ⅛ tsp. granulated garlic
- ⅛ tsp. nutmeg
- ¼ tsp. salt
- ⅛ tsp. white pepper

DIRECTIONS

Preheat oven to 425 degrees. Prebake the pie shell for 5 minutes. Remove from the oven and cool. Reduce oven temperature to 400 degrees.

In a large skillet, melt the butter over medium heat. Add the venison and cook until browned, stirring constantly. Transfer the venison to the pie shell. Distribute the bacon and chives over the venison followed by the mushrooms and cheese.

In a medium bowl, beat together the eggs and cream. Add the granulated garlic, nutmeg, salt and pepper, and mix well.

Place the pie shell on a baking tray. Pour the egg mixture into the pie shell and place in the oven. Bake for 25 to 30 minutes, or until top begins to brown. Let stand for 15 minutes before slicing.

SERVE WITH FRESH FRUIT AND CINNAMON TOAST.

BAKED PERCH WITH APRICOTS, DRIED CRANBERRIES AND OLIVES

SERVES 4

INGREDIENTS

- 2 lbs. boneless, skinless perch fillets
- 3 dried apricots and 1 tbsp. dried cranberries, soaked for 2 hours in ½ cup of cream sherry
- 1 stick butter
- ½ cup sliced Kalamata olives
- 3 green onions, thinly sliced
- 1 cup heavy cream
- 2 cups white wine
- 1 cup clam juice

DIRECTIONS

Drain the apricots and cranberries. Chop the apricots to the same size as the cranberries.

Fold and layer the perch fillets in a buttered baking dish. Top with the apricots, cranberries, olives and green onion. Mix the wine and clam juice together and pour over the fillets. Cover with foil and bake in a 350 degree oven for 12 to 15 minutes.

Remove the foil and pour the cooking liquid into a saucepan. Return the fish to the oven to keep warm. Bring the cooking liquid to a boil and reduce by one-half. Reduce heat to low and whisk in the cream and butter. Pour sauce over the fish. Serve with steamed vegetables.

FRUIT, BALANCED WITH SALTY ITEMS LIKE OLIVES OR CAPERS, IMPARTS A SWEET/SOUR FLAVOR PROFILE TO THE FISH.

PERCH PARMESAN

SERVES 4-6

INGREDIENTS

- **2 lbs. boneless, skinless yellow perch fillets**
- **1 cup olive oil**
- **3 cloves garlic, minced**
- **1½ cups Parmesan cheese, finely grated**
- **1½ cups cracker crumbs, finely processed**
- **2 tsp. Italian seasoning**

DIRECTIONS

Mix the olive oil and garlic in a large bowl. Add the perch and marinate 20 minutes, turning several times to coat all sides.

Place cheese, cracker crumbs and Italian seasoning in a large plastic bag and shake to mix. Place several fillets in the bag at a time to coat. Transfer to a well-oiled baking pan. Bake at 350 degrees for 12 to 14 minutes or until the fish flakes with a fork.

IF YOU HAPPEN TO HAVE A LOT OF PERCH, COAT THEM IN THE CHEESE MIXTURE AND FREEZE THEM INDIVIDUALLY FOR FUTURE USE.

SALMON EN CROUTE

SERVES 4

SERVE SALMON EN CROUTE WITH HOLLANDAISE SAUCE AND DELIGHT YOUR GUESTS AS THEY SAVOR THE STEAMY LICORICE FLAVOR OF THIS DISH.

INGREDIENTS

- **4 6-oz. pieces salmon fillets**
- **3 slices bacon, cut into ¼" dice**
- **1 tbsp. sweet butter**
- **3 tbsp. onion, diced**
- **1 clove garlic, minced**
- **2 tbsp. asiago cheese, shredded**
- **2 cups steamed spinach, all water removed**
- **1 oz. Pernod or pastis**
- **9 5"x5" puff pastry sheets**
- **1 egg, beaten**

DIRECTIONS

Sauté the bacon, onion and garlic in the butter, until bacon is slightly rendered and the onion is translucent. Remove pan from the heat and stir in the cheese, spinach and Pernod. Season to taste with salt and pepper. Chill mixture at least 1 hour before proceeding.

Place salmon fillets, skin side down, on work surface. Place ¼ cup of the spinach mixture on each fillet and roll into a cylinder. Chill at least 1 hour before proceeding.

Roll out 2 pieces of puff pastry large enough to cover a salmon roll overlapping by ½" on each side. Place salmon on 1 piece of the pastry and brush edges of pastry with beaten egg. Drape the 2nd piece of pastry over the salmon. Trim edges and seal by roll folding the edges. Repeat these steps for the remaining salmon rolls.

Cut decorative shapes from the remaining pastry piece. Brush top of pastry with beaten egg and place cutout on top of each salmon en croute. Bake at 400 degrees for 20 minutes or until golden brown.

BASS AND PASTA IN PARSLEY CREAM SAUCE

SERVES 4

INGREDIENTS

- 1 lb. boneless, skinless bass fillets, cut into bite-size pieces
- 1 medium onion, peeled, sliced and coarsely chopped
- 4 tbsp. butter
- 1½ cups heavy cream
- 3 tbsp. fresh parsley, chopped
- salt and pepper to taste
- 8 oz. dry pasta shells, cooked according to package directions
- 1 cup shredded provolone cheese

DIRECTIONS

Melt the butter in a large sauté pan. Add the onion and stir-fry until opaque. Add the cream and bass pieces. Simmer for 5 minutes or until the fish begins to flake. Adjust seasoning with salt and pepper. Add cook to 3 minutes, or until cheese begins to melt. Transfer to a heated serving bowl and serve immediately.

FOR ADDED FLAVOR, SPRINKLE WITH TOASTED ALMONDS OR PECANS.

ARKANSAS-STYLE PAN FISH

SERVES 4-6

INGREDIENTS

- **2 lbs. crappie fillets**
- **1 cup cornmeal**
- **1 cup pecan pieces**
- **1 cup seasoned breadcrumbs**
- **¼ teaspoon salt**
- **dash of cayenne pepper**
- **2 large eggs, well beaten**

DIRECTIONS

Place the cornmeal, pecans, salt, cayenne pepper and breadcrumbs in a food processor. Process until very fine. Dip the fillets in the egg and then the meal mixture.

Heat frying oil to 375 degrees. Fry several pieces of fish at a time until golden brown. Drain on a paper towel and keep warm in a 200 degree oven until ready to serve.

THIS COATING MIXTURE WORKS WELL FOR ALL KINDS OF FISH. MAKE EXTRA AND STORE IN AN AIRTIGHT CONTAINER OR BAGS IN THE FREEZER.

ENGLISH-STYLE FISH AND CHIPS

SERVES 6

INGREDIENTS

- 2 lbs. boneless, skinless fish fillets, your choice
- 2 cups self-rising flour
- ⅔ cup cold water
- ⅓ cup beer

- 1½ lbs. potatoes, peeled
- oil for deep frying
- lemon wedges
- malt vinegar

THE BATTER IN THIS RECIPE IS VERY SIMILAR TO A TEMPURA BATTER AND CAN BE USED WITH SHRIMP OR VEGETABLES, AS WELL AS THE FISH FILLETS.

DIRECTIONS

In a large bowl, mix a pinch of salt with the flour. Gradually whisk in the water and beer to make a smooth batter. Cover and set aside for at least 30 minutes.

Cut the potatoes lengthwise into slices ½" thick, then into ½" wide strips. Rinse under cold running water. Drain and dry well.

Heat the oil in a deep fryer or heavy fry pan to 300 degrees. Using a wire basket, fry the potatoes in small batches for 5 to 6 minutes, or until soft but not brown. Remove from oil and drain on paper towels.

Increase the oil temperature to 375 degrees. Stir the batter and coat the fish fillets, placing on a rack to drain excess batter.

Working in batches and using a basket, deep fry the fish for 6 to 8 minutes until the fish floats and is golden brown. Drain on paper towels and keep warm.

Again, working in batches, return the potatoes to the oil and fry for 2 to 3 minutes until golden brown and crisp. Drain and keep hot. Sprinkle with salt. Serve with malt vinegar and lemon wedges.

LAKE TROUT BAKED IN GRAPE LEAVES WITH OLIVE SALSA

SERVES 4

INGREDIENTS

- 4 6-oz. boneless, skinless lake trout fillets
- 1 16-oz. jar grape leaves
- ½ cup couscous
- 1 small jar roasted red pepper or pimento
- 1 tbsp. chopped cilantro
- 1 tbsp. chopped parsley
- 1 tbsp. lemon zest, chopped
- 1 tsp. minced garlic
- 1 tsp. chopped basil
- 2 tbsp. olive oil
- salt and pepper
- 4 orange slices
- 1 cup dry white wine
- 4 oz. feta cheese with basil and tomato
- 1 cup shredded lettuce

OLIVE SALSA

- 2 tbsp. minced onion
- ¼ cup Kalamata olives, pitted and chopped
- ¼ cup salad olives, pitted and chopped
- 3 tbsp. red wine vinegar
- 2 tsp. chopped oregano
- ¼ cup olive oil

DIRECTIONS

Soak grape leaves in 1 cup hot water for 5 minutes. Remove, unfold and drain.

Place couscous in a bowl an stir in m cup boiling water. Cover and let rest for 5 minutes. Fluff with a fork. Add the red peppers, cilantro, parsley, lemon zest, garlic, basil and olive oil. Season with salt and pepper to taste.

Season the fillets with salt and pepper and top each with 2 tablespoons of the couscous and an orange slice. Wrap each fillet with grape leaves and place in a roasting pan. Brush with olive oil, add the wine, cover and bake at 325 degrees for 15 to 20 minutes, basting occasionally.

While the fish is baking, combine all salsa ingredients in a small bowl.

IF GRAPE LEAVES ARE NOT AVAILABLE, USE BUTTERED SQUARES OF ALUMINUM FOIL TO FORM INDIVIDUAL BAKING PACKETS.

TEMPURA CATFISH

SERVES 4

INGREDIENTS

- **8 catfish fillets**
- **1 cup flour**
- **frying oil, heated to 375 degrees**

THIS SHOULD BE YOUR GO-TO BATTER FOR VEGETABLES, MEAT AND FISH.

TEMPURA BATTER

- **1½ cups flour**
- **1 tsp. salt**
- **1 tbsp. canola oil**
- **2 egg yolks, beaten**
- **¾ cups beer**

DIRECTIONS

In a large bowl, mix together the flour, salt, oil and eggs. Gradually add the beer. Cover and refrigerate 3 to 4 hours.

Dust the fillets with flour, then dip in batter just before frying, shaking off any excess. Fry fillets until they are light brown and they float. Keep fillets warm in a 200 degree oven until ready to serve.

BAKED SUCKER CASSEROLE

SERVES 4-6

INGREDIENTS

- **3 cups boneless, skinless steamed sucker (approximately 2 lbs.), cut into bite-size pieces**
- **½ cup chopped onion**
- **½ cup chopped celery**
- **¼ cup butter**
- **3 tbsp. flour**
- **2 cups milk or cream**
- **1 can peas and carrots, drained**
- **salt and pepper to taste**

DIRECTIONS

Melt the butter and sauté the onion and celery for 3 to 4 minutes, or until slightly browned. Reduce the heat and stir in the flour. Gradually whisk in the milk, stirring until thickened. Season to taste with salt and pepper. Stir in the peas and carrots and add the fish.

Place mixture in a buttered loaf pan and bake at 325 degrees for 20 to 30 minutes. Serve over buttered noodles or toast points.

PRIOR TO STEAMING THE FISH, REMOVE ANY FAT FROM THE BELLY AND DORSAL FIN AREA OF THE FILLET. STEAMING ALLOWS FOR EASY REMOVAL OF THE SKIN AND ANY REMAINING BONES.

ONE-POT CISCO MEAL

SERVES 2-4

INGREDIENTS

- **2 15-oz. cans stewed tomatoes**
- **1 lb. boneless, skinless cisco fillets**
- **2 cups cooked rice, mixed with 2 cups tomato juice**
- **salt and pepper**

DIRECTIONS

Place stewed tomatoes in a heavy sauté pan and bring to a boil. Reduce heat to medium and season to taste with salt and pepper. Lay the cisco fillets on top of the tomatoes, spread the rice over the fish and cover. Cook over medium heat until the tomatoes start to simmer, 5 to 8 minutes. Reduce heat to medium-low, cover and cook for 15 to 20 minutes without removing the lid.

Serve when fish flakes and the rice is hot.

ADD COOKED VEGETABLES, SUCH AS CORN OR PEAS, TO THE RICE TO ROUND OUT THIS DISH.

PIKE WITH BACON IN CREAM SAUCE

SERVES 4-6

INGREDIENTS

- **2 lbs. boneless, skinless pike fillets**
- **8 slices bacon, cooked and chopped**
- **1 cup white wine**
- **1 cup water**
- **1 tsp. salt**
- **1 tbsp. lemon juice**
- **1 can condensed cream of celery soup**
- **2 cups heavy cream**
- **1 cup mild salsa**

DIRECTIONS

Place fish in a large saucepan with water, salt and wine. Bring to a boil, reduce heat to low, cover and simmer for 10 to 12 minutes, or until the fish flakes with a fork. Remove the fish from the liquid, cool and break into bite-size pieces.

In a 2-quart pot, combine the soup and cream. Heat over low heat, stirring constantly, until bubbly. Stir in the bacon and salsa and fold in the fish. Heat until hot. Spoon over steamed rice or wide noodles.

REDUCE THE AMOUNT OF CREAM TO ONE CUP AND USE THIS AS A PARTY DIP WITH NACHOS OR TACO CHIPS.

CORNISH PASTIES

SERVES 4

PASTRY DOUGH

- 2⅔ cups flour
- ½ lb. cold sweet butter, cut into small pieces
- ½ cup ice water

FILLING

- 1½ cups meat (venison, beef, pork etc.), cut in 1" cubes
- 2 tbsp. flour
- 2 tbsp. olive oil
- ½ cup white wine
- ¼ tsp. minced garlic
- 1 tbsp. Dijon mustard
- 1 tsp. brown sugar
- ½ cup blanched diced turnip
- ½ cup blanched diced carrot
- ½ cup blanched diced rutabaga
- ½ cup par-boiled diced white potato
- ½ cup sautéed onion
- 1 cup sliced mushrooms

CORNISH MINERS WHO SETTLED IN THE UPPER PENINSULA OF MICHIGAN IN THE MID-1800S FOUND THIS BAKED POCKET EASY TO TRANSPORT AND PERFECT FOR "DINING" IN THE CRAMPED, HOT IRON MINES. ORIGINALLY, THE PASTRY WAS MADE WITH LARD, AND MEAT WAS AN INSIGNIFICANT INGREDIENT IN AN ECONOMY WHERE THE AVERAGE WAGE WAS LESS THAN $30 PER MONTH. THIS RECIPE IS FOR A MORE FORMAL PARTY, COMPLETE WITH PLENTY OF CHOPPED MEAT, VEGETABLES AND A BUTTERY SHORTBREAD STAMPED WITH AN ELEGANT SEAL.

DIRECTIONS

Pastry Dough:

In a food processor bowl fitted with a metal blade, cut the butter into the flour by pulsing the blade. Turn the machine on constant power and slowly add the ice water in a steady stream. In less than 30 seconds, a ball will form. Stop the machine. Divide the dough into 8 equal portions. Wrap each in plastic wrap and refrigerate for at least one hour.

Filling:

In a heavy skillet, heat the olive oil over medium heat. Dust the meat with flour, add to heated oil and brown on all sides. Remove to a stainless steel bowl. Deglaze the skillet with wine and add the garlic, mustard and brown sugar. Pour this reduction over the meat and marinate at least one hour in the refrigerator.

Drain marinade from meat and reserve. Combine meat with vegetables.

Roll pastry dough into 7" rounds. Place one cup of the meat/vegetable mixture in the center. Spoon 2 tablespoons marinade on top. Place second round on top, like a sandwich. Fold and crimp seal the pastry. Place pasties on baking sheet. Brush with cold water or egg wash. Cut a small vent in the top. Bake in a preheated 350 degree oven for 20 to 25 minutes or until golden brown.

BARBECUED GOOSE

SERVES 2-4

INGREDIENTS

- 1 lb. raw goose per serving

BARBECUED GOOSE

- ¼ lb. butter
- 1 large onion, diced
- 4 cloves garlic, finely minced
- ¼ tsp. oregano
- ¼ tsp. cumin
- ¼ tsp. crushed rosemary
- ¼ tsp. salt
- ⅛ tsp. pepper
- ⅛ tsp. ginger
- 5-6 tbsp. chili powder
- 4 cups ketchup
- 6 oranges
- ½ cup dark molasses
- ⅛ cup vinegar

DRY RUB SEASONING

- 2 tbsp. salt
- ¼ cup dried onion
- 2 tbsp. cayenne pepper
- 1 tbsp. white pepper
- 2 tbsp. paprika
- 2 tbsp. dried basil
- 1 tbsp. dry mustard
- 1 tbp. ground cumin
- 1 tbsp. granulated garlic

DIRECTIONS

Barbecue Sauce:
In a 2-quart sauté or saucepan, melt the butter over medium heat. Add the onion and garlic and sauté until the onions are translucent. Add the dry spices and continue cooking for 3 minutes, stirring constantly.

Cut the oranges in half and squeeze the juice into the pan. Reserve the orange rinds. Simmer 2 minutes. Add the catsup, molasses and vinegar and mix thoroughly. Bring the mixture to a boil. Reduce heat to low and add the orange rinds. Cover and simmer for one hour. Remove the orange rinds and reserve for stuffing the goose.

Goose:
Preheat the oven to 450 degrees. Remove excess fat from body cavity. Season cavity with salt and pepper and stuff with orange rinds from barbecue sauce.

Season the outside of the goose with Dry Rub seasoning.

Place goose in roasting pan, breast side down on a rack. Reduce oven heat to 350 degrees. Cook, uncovered, 20 minutes per pound. Halfway through the cooking time, turn the goose breast side up. Baste with barbecue sauce during the last 30 minutes of cooking time.

BARBECUED GOOSE? HENRY SAYS, "I KNOW, I KNOW." JUST TRUST HIM ON THIS. WHEN HENRY LIVED IN SAN FRANCISCO BACK IN 1983, HE ENTERED THIS SAUCE IN THE SAN FRANCISCO EXAMINER'S "BEST BARBECUE SAUCE" CONTEST. HE WON. THE MILD, MOUTH-WATERING TANG MAKES THIS SAUCE A WINNER. PLUS, THE MAHOGANY GLAZED PRESENTATION IS WINNING CONVERTS ACROSS THE NORTHWOODS. SO, GO AHEAD. BARBECUE YOUR GOOSE.

RECIPE NOTES

RECIPE NOTES

RECIPE NOTES